Seven Keys to Understanding and Enduring Personal Trials

MY GOD
hath been my
SUPPORT

DAVID T. MORGAN, PhD

Covenant Communications, Inc.

Published by Covenant Communications, Inc.
American Fork, Utah

Printed in the United States of America
First Printing: January 2018

24 23 22 21 20 19 18   10 9 8 7 6 5 4 3 2 1

ISBN-13: 978-1-52440-492-5

MY GOD
hath been my
SUPPORT

ACKNOWLEDGMENTS

THE PROCESS OF WRITING AND publishing this book has been a long and blessed process. I have learned so much about writing, patience, faith, and the goodness of God that the journey has been a greater blessing than the destination. In some ways, this book is as much counsel for me as it is for the intended audience. We all struggle with challenges, and I truly hope these concepts will help bring happiness and joy to those who read and apply them. There are so many who have been helpful in the experience of bringing this book from my mind to your hands, and I name only a few.

I'm thankful to those who provided thoughtful reviews of early manuscripts, including Deena Morgan, Janae Smith, Spencer Morgan, Marilyn Harker, and Sallie Nielson. Others provided emotional support and encouragement along the way, including all of my brothers and sisters, their spouses, and my parents. I'm very appreciative of the kind guidance and direction received from Scott Richards, Lane Fischer, Dan Judd, and Boyd Ware. I am especially thankful to Bonnie Brien, whose superb editorial skills transformed initial drafts into an excellent manuscript. I am also appreciative to Kami Hancock, Sam Millburn, Stephanie Lacy, Christina Marcano, and Robby Nichols of Covenant Communications, who have been great colleagues and provided excellent support.

I'd like to thank my children, who have been patient with me as I have stressed and worried during the past two years. Lastly, I thank my remarkable wife, who is my superior in every way. She constantly inspires me to be better and reach higher. She has been my sounding board from start to finish with this project. Her insights and support have been indispensable. I love you, Kristyn. Thank you for being so kind and supportive.

PREFACE

My wife and I are the proud parents of six wonderful children. We are faithful members of The Church of Jesus Christ of Latter-day Saints and have been blessed to enjoy understanding of the gospel and being active in the Church all our lives. As our five sons and one daughter grew older, we talked regularly about the importance of serving a mission when the time came. Sending our oldest son to the Provo Missionary Training Center (MTC) in Provo, Utah, was a proud moment for the whole family. It was the beginning of what we hoped would be a long period of faithful missionary service.

About four weeks into his stay at the MTC, we received a surprise phone call from our son. He was struggling with emotional issues, and one of the mental health counselors suggested he call home for support. My wife and I talked with him for about an hour and had a good conversation. We worried that he might want to come home, but he reassured us of his commitment and desire to serve.

Four weeks after that incident, I received another phone call from the MTC. This call was different. It was a Friday afternoon. Our son was scheduled to fly from the MTC to his assigned mission the following Monday. On the other end of the line was one of the MTC district presidents. He said, "I need you and your wife to get on a plane and get here right now." He informed me our son had suffered a serious emotional setback and would be coming home. Minimal details were provided, but I was told my wife and I would receive more information in person.

I called my wife to tell her what had just happened and then booked tickets on the next flight to Salt Lake City, Utah. We made arrangements to meet with the district president the next morning. The sixteen hours that followed were some of the longest of my life. My mind raced, and my heart overflowed with emotion. I thought of things I could say to the district president to change his mind. Surely they had overreacted. I prayed they would allow our son to stay in the MTC and go to his mission as previously arranged. As we met with the district president and our son the next morning, it became clear that there would be no change in plans. He informed me our son's emotional difficulties had increased to the point where he would not be permitted to remain on a mission for the Church. He would be extended a clinical medical release and could possibly return to mission service following a period of emotional rehabilitation. The outcome was clear and non-negotiable; our son would leave with us. The three of us flew back home that day.

Thus began the hardest year of our lives to that point. The next twelve months were filled with anger, sadness, questioning, guilt, shame, and regret. However, those same twelve months were also filled with understanding, repentance, joy, acceptance, humility, love, and peace. In retrospect, our family experienced valuable growth. During that year, our son was able to better prepare himself. He ultimately returned to the mission field with great success. I am convinced the Lord intended for us to go through those challenges for our learning and spiritual growth.

In pondering this experience, I learned that life is full of challenges and suffering. No one is exempt; we all experience difficulty. We often spend a lot of energy trying to convince others nothing is wrong. We broadcast the image that we are sailing through mortality without any problems. However, I think if the truth were really told, we would all openly acknowledge our lives are very difficult at times. Marriages struggle, children are disobedient, finances are tight, illnesses are chronic, and self-doubt is relentless. We fight against the same challenges time after time, wondering if we will ever be able to make lasting change.

With this book, I intend to help readers understand that struggling through life is not only common but also one of the core purposes of our mortal existence. We are here in life to try to succeed. Along the way we will encounter periodic failure and learn from our trials. All these experiences will help us gain a greater appreciation of the Atonement of Jesus Christ. As we begin to understand the reasons behind our challenges and reach out to the Savior for support, we will experience a greater measure of peace and solace.

INTRODUCTION

As a psychologist, I have had experience and training regarding the concept of self-esteem. Self-esteem is commonly defined as having respect for one's capacities and for oneself, including a feeling of confidence. Low self-esteem is a very common occurrence among individuals. How can we increase the amount of respect we have for ourselves? Society spends billions and billions of dollars a year seeking a solution, usually in vain. Having been fortunate enough to receive my doctoral training at Brigham Young University, I was able to study the gospel of Jesus Christ in connection with my psychology curriculum. As I have read and studied the scriptures throughout the years, I have concluded that the concept of self-esteem the world uses is different than the type of self-concept God wants us to achieve.

If you look up *Self-Esteem* in the Topical Guide to the scriptures, you will not find any scripture references. However, you will be referred to other topics as follows: "Man, a Spirit Child of Heavenly Father; Man, Potential to Become like Heavenly Father; Worth of Souls." Man's definition of self-esteem seems to be about having respect for our *own* selves and our *own* abilities. It has more to do with what *we* can do to better ourselves with our *own* efforts, without relying on others. Yet from a spiritual perspective, the concept of becoming greater or more confident is not about what we can do on our own but is about partnering with God and gaining strength through Him. The scriptures record the following regarding such confidence:

> Let thy bowels also be full of charity towards all men, and to the household of faith, and let virtue garnish thy thoughts unceasingly; then shall thy confidence wax strong in the presence of God; and the doctrine of the priesthood shall distil upon thy soul as the dews from heaven. (D&C 121:45)

Note how the scripture indicates that confidence increases in the presence of God as one becomes more obedient and pure in heart. Being full of charity, faith, and virtue contribute to this process. Relying solely on our abilities and ideas tends to meet with frustration and failure. The lasting emotional security and self-confidence that God wants for us requires reliance upon Him and His commandments.

In the 1978 motion picture *Superman*, starring Christopher Reeve, Lois Lane is a reporter with the *Daily Planet* who is granted an exclusive interview with Superman. He meets her at her penthouse apartment in Metropolis, where she asks him a number of background questions. When the interview turns to the topic of Superman's flying ability, he invites her to fly with him. She takes his hand, and they ascend into the night sky together. At first she is scared, clinging to the Man of Steel tightly. However, as she starts to become more confident, she relaxes her grip. At one point they are flying side by side, arms outstretched, holding hands. Lois continues to loosen her grip and after a while is just barely touching Superman's fingers with her own. As her confidence increases, she lets go of him entirely. The moment her fingers lose contact with his, she immediately falls. Screaming in terror, she plummets toward the earth. In dramatic fashion, Superman flies to her rescue, scoops her up in his arms, and saves her from certain death.

The reality is this: Lois Lane cannot fly. She has no ability to do so. She does not have the same superhero pedigree as Superman. She is a regular mortal, and her best bet to fly would be to contact a good travel agent. However, when she partners with the superhero, she is able to temporarily partake of his powers. As long as she holds on to him, she can fly. As soon as she lets go, she returns to her own mortal abilities.

Our relationship with Heavenly Father has similarities to that of Lois and Superman's. Imagine being able to join forces with a being more powerful than an infinite number of superheroes! When we are obedient to His commandments and partner with Him, we are able to do amazing things. We are able to reach beyond our natural capacities. When we "release our grasp" with God, we are left to our own devices. We often find life to be much more difficult as a result. As such, the world's concept of self-esteem cannot really exist in a gospel framework, because we were never intended to get through life relying simply on our own abilities. Rather, the concept of spiritual confidence is much better suited to the idea of how we can improve ourselves in this life. As we join hands with our Father in Heaven, we will begin to experience the joy and assurance He has always intended for us. He wants us to return confidently, having done our part while relying on the power of the Atonement of Jesus Christ. Developing greater spiritual strength will help us better understand and endure the trials and difficulties we face in life.

The principal chapters of this book each contain a key concept related to how we can develop greater spiritual strength. That concept is restated at the ends of those chapters. There are also specific questions designed to help you reflect on your own experience, ponder where you are in the development of heavenly characteristics, and consider changes you can make in your own life. If you truly seek for direction in how to improve your life, the Holy Ghost will provide individualized and ideal feedback regarding potential paths of change. Following the promptings of the Holy Ghost will improve your quality of life and lead to greater happiness and peace. It will also help you be more confident as you deal with challenges and will give you an increased depth of understanding of Heavenly Father's plan for you.

CHAPTER 1
The Truth of the Matter

WE ALL HAVE BAD DAYS.

I'm not just talking about days when your favorite sports team loses or when the kids have a minor tantrum after you walk past the candy aisle in the grocery store. I'm talking about those days when the *best* thing that happens is the tantrum in the candy aisle followed by a full-blown in-store meltdown. The two oldest children are fighting, the baby is screaming, and the toddler breaks loose and runs through the parking lot with a loaded diaper. The drive home is full of yelling and crying followed by the bottom falling out of one of the grocery bags during unloading. The day is capped off by trying to put all the kids to bed at 6:30 P.M. (even though it won't be dark until nine). I'm talking about those days when your dinner consists of a tear-filled bowl of ice cream and dessert is polishing off the remaining half gallon.

Then there are other times when such "bad days" seem like nothing compared to serious life challenges. We hear of friends losing their jobs or getting diagnosed with some dread disease. For individuals who face such difficulties, "bad days" often turn into bad weeks and bad years, with no apparent hope on the horizon. We feel badly for them yet are secretly grateful our lives do not consist of such chronic difficulties. We feel blessed to not have such trials. These experiences naturally invite the question, "Why do some people have serious challenges while others do not?" I admit, there are times in life when my answer to that question has been, "Well, perhaps they were not keeping the commandments like they should have." I think we sometimes believe we have successfully avoided these types of challenges due to good behavior on our part. We may believe that if we are just righteous enough and keep the commandments, we will not have to pass through serious consequences.

At times we may look at those who have major challenges in life and think, *I wonder what they did, or perhaps didn't do, in order to run into such difficulties?* We create fictions in our minds to explain to ourselves why God did not intervene and protect them against those hardships. Were they lacking in faith? Were they untrue to their covenants? Perhaps there were so many sins of omission that simply piled up to the point where God could not deliver these people from the consequences? Jesus's disciples of old had the same question. In their travels, they encountered a man who had been born blind. "And his disciples asked him, saying, Master, who did sin, this man, or his parents, that he was born blind? Jesus answered, Neither hath this man sinned, nor his parents: but that the works of God should be made manifest in him" (John 9:2–3). This man's trial was apparently in place so that Jesus could heal him; it had nothing to do with any sinful or neglectful behavior on the part of the man or his parents.

Sometimes we believe that consistent obedience to the commandments is some sort of protective guarantee against chronic hardship. I'm not sure why we think this at times, but I believe it may have to do with a desire for control and a fear of failure. We want to hedge our bets to ensure we will not have serious trials, and we somehow believe that obedience to gospel principles will create such a buffer. Even though I have had this belief at times, it has not held true in my own experience. Furthermore, I have not found it to be accurate in the lives of my friends. I have not found it to be accurate in the stories told of prophets and other faithful saints. For generations, prophets have taught we will be blessed if we will keep the commandments. That is completely true. However, being "blessed" does not always mean what we think it means. It does not always mean things go smoothly. Following are a few examples of individuals who were extremely righteous yet were faced with tremendous personal challenges.

Eve: A woman so righteous she was chosen to be the mother of the human race. One of her children was so wicked that not only did he murder his brother but he also consistently chose evil over good and was eventually doomed to wander the earth as a vagabond (see Moses 5:36–39).

Lehi: A prophet of God, chosen to escape the destruction of Jerusalem and take his family to inherit a land of promise. Two of his children were "murderers in [their] hearts" (1 Nephi 17:44) who tried to kill their brother on multiple occasions and ended up establishing a nation that was spiritually challenged for generations.

Sarah: Married to Father Abraham, who was foreordained to be one of God's leaders (see Abraham 3:23). After receiving the promise that she and her husband would be the source of an innumerable posterity, she continued to be childless and barren for decades. Finally, after miraculously giving birth to a son in her old age, she discovered the Lord commanded her husband to take the child's life as a sacrifice.

Mosiah: A righteous Book of Mormon king and leader who led his people in peace (see Mosiah 6:6–7). Four of his sons chose to reject his example. They turned to evil works and were described as the "very vilest of sinners" (Mosiah 28:4). His sons actively tried to destroy the progress of the Church and lead others into sin (see Mosiah 27:10).

Esther: An orphan who experienced a remarkable change of fate to become wife to the king of Persia. She discovered that her entire people, the Jews, were going to be slaughtered by members of the Persian kingdom. She took her life into her own hands by approaching the king without invitation to beg for the lives of her people (see Esther 1–5).

Job: A man described as "perfect and upright" (Job 1:1) in keeping the commandments who experienced considerable tragedies, including the significant and traumatic loss of family members, his health, and possessions.

Abinadi: A bold prophet of the Lord who dutifully followed a commandment to preach repentance to a wicked people (see Mosiah 12:1). He was imprisoned because of his obedience. When he stayed true to his mission despite being given the chance for freedom if he would deny his own words, he was executed by being burned alive.

Emma Smith: Described by the Lord Himself as an "elect lady" (D&C 25:3). The faithful wife of the Prophet Joseph Smith was driven from her home multiple times, experienced the premature death of several children, and suffered the cold-blooded murder of her husband.

Surely there are many other examples throughout history of the righteous being tried and tested. Perhaps you are thinking of similar experiences with such trials in your life. After doing your best to keep the commandments of God and to honor your covenants, things still go wrong (including children being wayward, facing unemployment, being afflicted with sickness, having marital problems, etcetera). Some of the best people you know have experienced serious setbacks in life despite their ongoing efforts to do what is right. Disobedience does not seem to be the cause of their challenges. On the contrary, their lives appear to be exemplary in many aspects.

Based on the actual experiences of human beings as opposed to erroneous yet sometimes popular belief, we can safely conclude the following: Those who faithfully keep the commandments of God will very likely experience trial, suffering, and difficulty that can at times be almost too great to bear.

While this statement may be discouraging, we can gain a better perspective once we understand the reasons for our trials and difficulties. Describing opposition and challenges, Lehi explained the following:

> For it must needs be, that there is an opposition in all things. If not so . . . righteousness could not be brought to pass, neither wickedness, neither holiness nor misery, neither good nor bad. Wherefore, all things must needs be a compound in one; wherefore, if it should be one body it must needs remain as dead, having no life neither death, nor corruption nor incorruption, happiness nor misery, neither sense nor insensibility. (2 Nephi 2:11)

By experiencing the negative, we learn to appreciate the positive (see Moses 6:55). This suggests part of our experience in life is going to be difficult, regardless of how obedient we are. Blessings do come to the faithful, but the timing and nature of such blessings can be challenging to understand. While obedience yields blessings, some blessings do not come for a very long time. Some blessings may even come in the form of trials and challenges. Your loving Father in Heaven blesses you with difficulties for your eventual benefit and growth. Sometimes we have a hard time seeing them as such.

I believe that before we came to Earth, we each sat down with our Father in Heaven in a personal interview. He explained what our mortal experience would be like. He outlined the trials we would face and how they would be perfectly designed for our optimal growth. We accepted His personalized plan for us and rejoiced in the knowledge that we could return to be with Him. When we came to Earth and crossed the veil, we forgot all we had learned in our premortal life. Our forgetfulness is evident when we question the purpose behind our trials. I think God feels sad when we blame Him for our difficulties. He tries to help us remember and realize the perfection in every step of His design.

We are not the first to have gone through trials and difficulties. Consider the accounts of those who have gone before us and how we can benefit from their examples. As we study their lives and experiences, we can learn how better to face our own challenges with faith and hope. Let's learn from the life of another prophet who endured great hardship despite his faithful keeping of commandments and covenants.

CHAPTER 2
"O Wretched Man That I Am"

NEPHI, THE SON OF LEHI, was highly blessed by the Lord. As a young man, he received a witness of the truth. He lived very comfortably in Jerusalem. Had he remained there, he would have likely continued to live very comfortably for the rest of his days. All of that changed with his father's calling to become a prophet of God.

While still a young man and inexperienced in the ways of the world, Nephi had to leave his comfort and wealth and flee into the wilderness with his family as fugitives. After traveling through a dangerous desert, he and his brothers were required to return to Jerusalem to obtain a sacred record. This experience involved long days of difficult travel. As part of this journey, Nephi had his life threatened by a ruthless leader, was physically assaulted by his brothers, and had to kill a man in order to obey the commands of God.

Their travels led them to the ocean, where God commanded Nephi to build a ship to facilitate crossing the sea. Nephi labored diligently to complete this task. He became frustrated at his brothers' lack of faith as they withheld their support and assistance. Eventually his brothers tried to kill him, yet Nephi was miraculously protected by the power of God. Ultimately, they completed the ship and embarked on their ocean voyage. Shortly after starting their journey seaward, his brothers engaged in very disobedient behavior on the ship. Nephi confronted them and demanded they stop. They tied him up and continued their reveling, completely unrepentant for having treated their brother with such harshness. A huge storm arose that threatened the lives of everyone on board. Nephi's brothers still refused to untie him, and he remained in this condition for several days. It was not until his brothers feared for their own lives that they released Nephi and the storm ceased.

After arriving on the shores of the Americas, Nephi's brothers resumed their complaints. Their father, Lehi, rebuked them and gave them his last counsel prior to his death. Shortly thereafter, Lehi died. This was a very difficult time for Nephi. Not only had he lost his father but his spiritual leader as well. He was left to try to lead a broken people while assuming the mantle of the prophet. In such trying times, his brothers were critical of his efforts. They threatened his life such that Nephi and his followers had to flee for their own safety. Amid his grief and suffering, Nephi cried out, "O wretched man that I am! Yea, my heart sorroweth because of my flesh; my soul grieveth because of mine iniquities. I am encompassed about, because of the temptations and the sins which do so easily beset me. And when I desire to rejoice, my heart groaneth because of my sins . . ." (2 Nephi 4:17–19).

Having just reviewed the history of this great prophet, I presume most of us would not consider him a "wretched man." This was the man who said, "I will go and do the things which the Lord hath commanded" (1 Nephi 3:7). This was the man who, when directed to build a ship (something he had never done before), didn't question but simply asked, "Whither shall I go that I may find ore to molten, that I may make tools to construct the ship . . . ?" (1 Nephi 17:9). This was the man who faithfully created a second set of records, having no idea why this should be done. He followed inspiration and stated it was "a wise purpose in [the Lord], which purpose [he knew] not" (1 Nephi 9:5).

Does this sound like a disobedient man? Someone easily beset by sins and temptations? Someone who could not rejoice in his behavior because of his sinful ways?

Nephi's trials seemed to culminate to the point where he cried out in frustration. This is understandable, considering the many difficulties he had experienced. It is particularly understandable in light of the multiple challenges in his life at that specific time. I assume we have all experienced similar moments at some point. Our Father in Heaven knows we will have such days; they are part of the plan. He is there to strengthen us and help us through these difficult times. If life's normal challenges were the only things we had to deal with, that would be difficult enough. However, our Father in Heaven isn't the only one trying to influence us during these moments of trouble. Satan also tries to influence us, with deceit and criticism. When we experience difficulty, the adversary does his best to beat us down and create a sense of personal failure. I can only imagine what he must have told Nephi in the moment of this particular trial:

"You're not good enough to be a prophet."

"There's no way you can adequately follow in the footsteps of your father; how can you emulate such a great example?"

"Your own brothers won't even listen to you; how do you expect to be their leader?"

"How can you teach others the way of righteousness when you yourself continue to struggle? Your hypocrisy will show."

Lucifer has similar things to say to each of us during times when we struggle. It is his goal to make us feel miserable: as miserable as he is, if possible (see 2 Nephi 2:27). Although his statements are founded on lies, sometimes we feel compelled to believe them. For example, some have difficulty accepting compliments, but they quickly embrace criticism. Have you ever had that experience? If someone pays you a compliment for a job well-done, do you say things like, "It wasn't that hard," or, "Anyone could have done that," thus effectively rejecting the compliment? Yet when someone criticizes your well-meaning behavior, do you sometimes accept the criticism as true?

We tend to put our best self forward and hide our weaknesses. We don't want others to see them, fearing rejection if they knew "how we really are." Most people have no idea of our challenges and difficulties. The only individuals who actually know all our weaknesses and frailties are Heavenly Father and Jesus Christ. They have a complete knowledge of all our sins and shortcomings, yet their acceptance of us is complete. They are always willing to help us. They hate sin yet love the sinner. They are the complete opposite of Satan. If the only individuals who truly know all our negative attributes are the same who love us unconditionally, shouldn't we be a little easier on ourselves?

While serving as a member of the Presiding Bishopric, Elder Richard C. Edgley said:

> Who are we going to believe in our search for happiness and well-being? Will it be Satan, the author of all lies and deceit, whose single objective is to destroy us? Or are we going to believe a loving Heavenly Father, who is the source of all truth and happiness, whose sole objective is rewarding us with His eternal love and joy?[1]

When the argument is made in that form, it seems clear we would never want to accept Satan's lies, just as we would never trust someone who had routinely harmed and cheated us. Yet Satan is very subtle, and we often believe his deceptions without realizing we have sided with the "enemy of [our] soul[s]" (2 Nephi 4:28). The truth is we are all children of God. We all struggle with weakness. Heavenly Father loves us for our goodness, and He loves us for our potential. He is merciful with our weakness. He provides ample time and opportunity for growth through learning and change through repentance.

---

1   Richard C. Edgley, "Satan's Bag of Snipes," *Ensign*, Nov. 2000, 43.

So it was with Nephi. He was a very good man, but he was a mortal man as well. As such, he struggled with issues from time to time. Satan capitalized on those struggles and succeeded in getting him to be critical of himself. In the agony of the moment, Nephi accused himself of being a "wretched man." This accusation was completely untrue, but it was still the way Nephi felt at the time. Our experiences are similar. We are good people who struggle for self-acceptance on occasion. Many of us have cried out in the dark and passed self-judgment that is harsh and untrue. In some ways, we know *exactly* how Nephi felt in that moment. Although our life experiences differ from his, the resulting emotional experience can be quite similar. "O wretched man/woman that I am!" may be a common cry for many of us.

Fortunately, we have the insights and thoughts of Nephi to help us correct our own negative self-talk. Following his statement of being a "wretched man," Nephi begins to reflect on some of the blessings he has received. He is able to reverse his negative feelings with the comfort and confidence provided by the Spirit of God. Some may say, "Well, of course *Nephi* could overcome his negative thoughts. He was a prophet of God. What chance do I have, as a regular person?"

I am fully confident that God is no respecter of persons. He loves you as much as he loved Nephi and will help you just as He helped him. The spiritual truths that Nephi used to overcome his challenges are readily available to all of us. Just as Nephi partnered with God to manage his difficulties, you can do the same. It doesn't matter if you are a prophet or not; once you take God's hand and accept His grace along the path of your trials, your ultimate success is guaranteed. The following chapters detail seven key strategies Nephi used as he described how he coped with personal challenges. They are good resources for us as well.

CHAPTER 3
"I Know in Whom I Have Trusted"

Why do we sometimes see the commandments as a burden?
Why do we sometimes not feel we can trust our Father in Heaven?

As NEPHI REFLECTED ON HIS own experience, he felt to "groan" because of the sins he believed he had committed (see 2 Nephi 4:18–19). It is important to note that Nephi was a prophet of God; he was likely not guilty of grievous sins. It is more likely he was feeling particularly discouraged in the midst of personal challenges. However, he was able to gain comfort through the following line of thinking: "I know in whom I have trusted. My God hath been my support; he hath led me through mine afflictions in the wilderness; and he hath preserved me upon the waters of the great deep" (2 Nephi 4:19–20). The first strategy Nephi appeared to use to manage his trials was to have a strong trust in our Father in Heaven and His Son Jesus Christ.

Nephi's reflections in 2 Nephi 4 are often referred to as the Psalm of Nephi. It was written after the death of Lehi, which happened after the family had arrived in the promised land. For reference, here is a recap of what had transpired to that point:

- Lehi's life was threatened in Jerusalem, and the family escaped.
- Nephi and his brothers went *back* to Jerusalem to retrieve sacred records from a murderous man.
- After returning to their parents, Nephi and his brothers went back *again* to Jerusalem to persuade Ishmael and his family to come with them.
- Nephi was tied up and left for dead in the desert and then rescued by the power of God.
- Due to a lack of hunting implements, the family suffered without food in the wilderness for a time.

- As he tried to build a seaworthy ship with homemade tools, Nephi's brothers attempted to kill him; he was saved by the power of God.
- Nephi was tied up by his brothers after embarking on the voyage. A serious storm threatened the group to the point of near-destruction. Only when Laman and Lemuel feared drowning did they untie Nephi, after which the Lord calmed the storm.

Perhaps that gives a little more background to Nephi's statement about being "led through [his] afflictions in the wilderness" and "preserved . . . upon the waters of the great deep" (2 Nephi 4:19–20). Lehi's family experienced considerable distress and challenges on their journey from Jerusalem to the Americas. Some of these challenges were literally life-threatening. Although their challenges were far more physically dangerous than the challenges faced by most of us today, they were not necessarily any less stressful. As Nephi remembered and reflected on the goodness of God throughout his days, he was able to process some of his negative feelings and gain some relief.

It was probably easy for Nephi to become depressed and discouraged after the death of his father. Serious trials typically provide fuel for personal doubt. In the midst of his difficulties, Nephi seemed to question his capacities. His doubts contributed to his lament of being a "wretched man" (2 Nephi 4:17). However, as Nephi started to remember the great things the Lord had done for him, he began to have a clearer sense of his reality.

I have found the same principle works for us today. Many times, when we are discouraged or worried, we tend to focus on something specific and negative. Such discouragement and worry then leads to additional negative beliefs, often growing in scale and consequence. Consider this possible situation as an example: Your boss provides some negative feedback regarding your portion of a project recently completed. You react with sadness and disappointment. You start to think, *The boss has been extra critical lately; the company has been laying some people off as well; I bet I'm the next to go.* Your thinking continues. *If I lose my job, there's no way we can survive. We don't have enough savings; we'll lose the house and have to move.* At this point, you become panicked, with thoughts of relocation and the impact this will have on your situation.

Here is another hypothetical example: One of your children fails an exam at school. You react with sadness and disappointment. As you discuss the situation with the teacher, you discover your child hasn't been doing his homework and is distracted during class. You start to think, *This is just the beginning; there's no way he'll get into college with this attitude. His chances for success are minimal.*

Your thinking continues. *Without a college education, he'll be a failure; we'll have to support him the rest of our lives. Where did we go wrong?* At this point, you are depressed with thoughts of failure and filled with doubts about your abilities as a parent.

Each of these examples is most likely an exaggeration of reality, fueled by fear and despair. While it is true that each situation began with an *actual* negative event, the thinking that followed was unrealistic and was out of proportion. Here are more accurate lines of thinking for such situations:

- *Yes, the boss has been critical, but I just received a great performance review. He's probably just having a bad day. I'll see how he feels tomorrow.*
- *True, my son just failed a test and is having some problems in class, but he is only in the first grade and will probably figure things out. With a little help and support, we can turn this around.*

We experience depressing and worrisome situations on a regular basis. Too much focus on the negative tends to yield depression and anxiety. Putting such situations in a proper context can help dispel serious negative reactions. We should consider as many angles as possible and gather plenty of information *before* coming to a conclusion. *In almost every case*, there is more good than bad in our lives. However, a myopic focus on the negative can lead us to believe otherwise.

Nevertheless, we will have struggles and challenges regardless of the positive attitude we try to have in our lives. There will be days that are difficult and discouraging. Going back to Nephi's original statement in this chapter, he said, "I know in whom I have trusted. My God hath been my support" (2 Nephi 4:19–20). Trusting in God is essential in this life. Many believe in God and believe He has all power. Some fail to make the transition to understanding how this applies to their personal situation.

Consider the time in Nephi's life when his brothers tied him up on a boat. Nephi had been commanded to build a ship. After the construction was finished, he and his family boarded for the long journey to the promised land. Many days later, Laman and Lemuel and some of their companions started to misbehave "with much rudeness" (1 Nephi 18:9). Nephi confronted them and was subsequently tied and bound by Laman and Lemuel. It is interesting to note how Laman and Lemuel, probably just a few short weeks or months before this, actually attempted to *worship* Nephi because of the way in which the power of God had come upon him (see 1 Nephi 17:55). Yet, now, they had tied him up and treated him with disdain and contempt. How quickly they seemed to forget their previous feelings and experience.

As Nephi remained tied and the rudeness of his brethren continued, a terrible storm began. The whole company was driven back on the water for four days. Nephi was physically bound this entire time and experienced the wrath of the storm. He suffered innocently, and his forward progress was halted. He knew his brothers were being punished for their behavior and the storm would cease if they would untie him. It wasn't until Laman and Lemuel feared for their lives that they decided to release Nephi. Once he was unbound, Nephi prayed to God, the storm ceased, and the journey progressed as intended.

During that frightening experience, Nephi was helpless, and he almost drowned in a mighty storm. It is interesting to note his reaction during this trial. "Nevertheless, I did look unto my God, and I did praise him all the day long; and I did not murmur against the Lord because of mine afflictions" (1 Nephi 18:16). This does not describe his attitude *before* being tied up or *after* the experience was over but *during* the actual trial. I have found it is fairly easy to say, "I'm sure I'll be ready for a trial if the Lord sees fit to give me one," or, "That trial was tough, but I'm glad I got the chance to go through it." It is much more difficult to be faithful and trust in God in the *midst* of trials. Trusting in God means we need to have faith and confidence that He is there for us. It means understanding His actions will be for our good.

Strangely, the natural man struggles to trust in God, though it seems logical that we should trust Him completely. For example, say you have a goal to summit a mountain you have never climbed before. While you have had some experience with mountain climbing, this particular peak is known to be challenging. Those who make it to the top enjoy amazing vistas and a sense of deep personal accomplishment. However, the climb is also known to be quite dangerous, resulting in loss of life for some. Local experts have been organized to provide guidance. They are the only ones who have sufficient skill to help the inexperienced reach the summit in safety.

As you organize your plans to make the climb, a particularly kind mountain-climbing expert approaches. The locals acknowledge him as the most advanced, experienced mountain guide they have ever known. Those who have climbed with him have never succumbed to the dangers of the mountain. He says to you, "I have been up and down this mountain more times than I can count. I have stood at the top many times and surveyed all the pitfalls, cliffs, and dangers. If you are willing, I will lead you up the mountain. I will provide you with a list of all essential equipment and will walk with you every step of the way. In essence,

I can guarantee your safety during this climb. In addition, my services are completely free. All you need to do is follow me, and I will ensure you will make it to the top safely and experience the incredible joy of reaching the summit."

Can you imagine anyone who would refuse such an offer? It seems foolish to even suggest such a scenario as the one that follows:

Climber: "I appreciate your offer of help, but I think I'll be fine on my own. I have a little experience. In fact, I've hiked a couple of small hills and have some old outdated equipment I plan to use, so I think I'm good to go."

Expert: "Are you sure? I know this mountain and can guarantee your safety. Many have died without appropriate guidance. How will you avoid the pitfalls and challenges?"

Climber: "I'm sure I'll be fine. The climb is probably easier than it looks. Thanks anyway."

Surely we would embrace the chance to have an experienced, confident guide at our side. Yet in our journey through mortality, we often seem to chafe against the idea of trusting our lives to such a companion. Imagine a slight variation on the previous scenario, relating to our mortal experience:

Heavenly Father: "Your journey through life is going to be treacherous. There are many challenges and difficulties to face as you learn how to control your impulses. In addition, Satan is real, and he is bent on your destruction. He will stop at nothing to ensure your failure. To guard against this, I'd like to be your guide. Please allow me to help you with decisions. I'll even give you suggestions and warnings to keep you safe from danger. If you are willing, I'll walk this dangerous path with you and keep you safe."

Mortal: "No thanks; I'm sure I'll be fine on my own. Besides, I tend to find commandments restrictive. I'd rather make my own choices without help and not have to be told what to do."

There may have been times in our lives when we have had a similar attitude. We may have difficulty trusting in God and accepting His help. It seems very natural to want to "be in charge," even when we could clearly benefit from assistance and direction. Perhaps we view it as a sign of weakness to depend upon another. Perhaps it is a symptom of pride. Regardless, the desire for control is a common condition of mortality. Wanting to be in control is not bad at all, but refusing to realize how and when to trust in God can lead to unnecessary grief.

Consider the example of Jesus Christ and how He made choices throughout His mortal life. He described His strategy as follows: "The Son can do nothing of himself, but what he seeth the Father do: for what things soever he doeth, these also doeth the Son likewise" (John 5:19). From this statement, we know that Jesus *always* followed the example and advice of His Father. He took full advantage of the counsel, direction, and guidance the Father provided. In fact, He never made a single choice that wasn't in harmony with the will of Heavenly Father. Hence, He lived a perfect life and was able to redeem all mankind. Jesus Christ fully trusted His Father in Heaven and navigated this life with grace and majesty. Indeed, He said, "My yoke is easy, and my burden is light" (Matthew 11:30). I don't believe that means He did not have challenges. Any serious study of His life will show that is not true. However, He was able to manage life's difficulties with greater ease having trusted in God.

The following statement from Elder Neal A. Maxwell of the Quorum of the Twelve Apostles, is instructive:

> The submission of one's will is really the only uniquely personal thing we have to place on God's altar. The many other things we "give," brothers and sisters, are actually the things He has already given or loaned to us. However, when you and I finally submit ourselves, by letting our individual wills be swallowed up in God's will, then we are really giving something to Him! It is the only possession which is truly ours to give![2]

The Savior gave to God the Father the only thing He really could have given. He completely submitted His will to the will of the Father. The results were glorious. As He is our perfect example, it follows that we should also learn to submit and learn to keep the commandments of God, trusting this will result in great benefits. We will experience blessings and happiness as we do this.

Sometimes we find it a challenge to submit our will to God due to things we have experienced in life. Some often feel that others control them or have had past experiences in which they have felt powerless. They don't want to give up power for fear of being weak or manipulated. As a result, they may have the same attitude toward the commandments. They don't want to obey, because they don't want to be "told what to do."

Years ago, I worked with a youth who had a number of behavioral problems. Eventually he was convicted of criminal behavior. He had been

---

2   Neal A. Maxwell, "Swallowed Up in the Will of the Father," *Ensign*, Nov. 1995, 24.

expelled from traditional high school and was on a "last-chance contract" with an alternative school. He also came from an extremely poor family, a fact he despised. He wanted a better life. To his credit, he was extremely intelligent. However, he was also very stubborn. He hated high school and scoffed at the idea of continuing on to college. For years, people had told him what to do, and he felt controlled at every turn.

I remember talking with him about his hatred of being poor and how I knew something of how he felt but perhaps on a smaller scale. I related stories about the times after my wife and I were first married. We were both in college, made six hundred dollars a month between the two of us, and our rent was more than fifty percent of our monthly take-home pay. Our grocery budget was a meager fifteen dollars a week. Each week we would go shopping, calculator in hand. We had to total up the items as we put them in the cart, trying to ensure we didn't go over budget. I recall walking down the cookie aisle, eyeing the name-brand treats. As I reached for the off-brand cookies, I longed for the day we could afford the more expensive and better-tasting varieties. Looking back, this seems pretty insignificant. Yet at the time, it was meaningful to me. These experiences motivated me to continue with college and pursue graduate studies. With the blessing of an advanced education and a solid career, I am pleased to report we are now able to purchase name-brand cookies without great concern.

I talked with this youth about how our choices now will either help or hinder our progress in the future. Most of the rules that apply to this life are unyielding. We must comply in order to achieve desired outcomes. This youth was not interested in my story and was even less interested in the idea of compliance in general. As I recall, he did not change his attitude, and we ultimately parted ways, leaving me with little hope for his future. I remember thinking he was going to face a long, difficult road unless he learned to do the things that would yield success. If we view commandments as a list of forbidden yet desirable behaviors, we will face a similar road.

The commandments come from our loving, eternal Father in Heaven. His *only purpose* is to help us return to Him and to give us everything He has (see Moses 1:39). He is full of compassion, mercy, and forgiveness. He loves us completely, regardless of our mistakes. As we return to Him after having strayed, He welcomes us back with open arms. He does this even when we have intentionally rebelled and refused His direction for years and years. He loves us so much that He sent His only perfect Son to redeem us. He stood by and watched others abuse, torture, and execute the only child who had never betrayed Him. *He did this for us.* "For God so loved the world, that he gave his only begotten Son, that whosoever believeth in him should not perish, but have everlasting life" (John 3:16). This is the Being we have been asked to trust. He is not a tyrant or a dictator, but a loving, infinite Being of incredible power and perfect knowledge.

Nephi stated, "I *know* in whom I have trusted" (2 Nephi 4:19; emphasis added). I think his use of the word *know* refers to his personal relationship with God. Nephi *knew* his Father in Heaven. He knew His character, he knew His commandments, and he trusted in His ability to preserve him regardless of the challenges he faced. Remember, *your Heavenly Father knows you*. We may have forgotten that relationship, but that does not mean He has. President Ezra Taft Benson described this idea as follows: "Nothing is going to startle us more when we pass through the veil to the other side than to realize how well we know our Father and how familiar His face is to us."[3] I believe we each enjoyed a wonderful, individual relationship with God before we came to this life. I'd like to think we had long interviews and conversations about our hopes and dreams. As it came time for us to leave His presence and come to Earth, I imagine we said a fond farewell. He likely asked us to please remember Him and to communicate often. Perhaps He even implored us to trust Him and follow His commandments. Yet here we are, sometimes viewing prayer as a chore and obedience as a burden. I have to think it breaks His heart a little bit each time we forget Him in our daily lives, when His whole existence is exclusively focused on us. Indeed, the scriptures record that "the heavens weep" when our relationship with Heavenly Father weakens (see Moses 7:28–40). And still, He stands ready to direct and guide us from the very time we will permit Him to do so, no matter how far we have strayed prior to that moment.

Quite frankly, there is really only one set of individuals in your life whom you can trust completely. They are your Father in Heaven and His Son Jesus Christ. *Everyone else*, regardless of their good intentions or their love for you, will probably let you down at some point. Some will do this innocently, some will do this intentionally, and some will do this with malice. However, your Heavenly Father and Savior will always be there for you, constant and secure. What a wonderful thing to realize, that amidst all the trials and turmoil of life, you have someone you can always trust. Remember this; trust Him first. Set aside any ego or rebellion and reach out to join hands with the most powerful and knowledgeable person in the universe. As the proverb wisely counsels, so should we always do: "Trust in the Lord with all thine heart; and lean not unto thine own understanding. In all thy ways acknowledge him, and he shall direct thy paths" (Proverbs 3:5–6).

---

3   Ezra Taft Benson, "Jesus Christ—Gifts and Expectations," *Ensign*, Dec. 1988, 6.

Key Concept 1

Come to know and trust Heavenly Father and the Savior.

QUESTIONS FOR SELF-REFLECTION

- How well can I trust people in general?
- How does it feel when I have to give up control?
- What can I do to better understand the character of my Father in Heaven?
- What can I do to better understand the Atonement of Jesus Christ?

CHAPTER 4
"He Hath Filled Me with His Love"

What motivated the Savior to die for us?
What does it mean to truly love someone?

As NEPHI CONTINUES TO REFLECT on his blessings and experiences with God, he makes the following statement: "He hath filled me with his love, even unto the consuming of my flesh" (2 Nephi 4:21). A closer examination of that statement indicates it does *not* say, "He has filled me with love." It says, "He has filled me with *his* love." The profound difference between these two statements can make a considerable difference when dealing with difficulties in life. Another strategy Nephi appeared to use to deal with difficulties was to deepen his understanding of God's love for him and strive to fill his heart with similar feelings.

Most everyone has experienced the feeling of love, and there are many different types. Love is often equated with romantic attraction, but I believe this is one of the most base and primal forms of this emotion. The deepest forms of love often have no romance at all. They transcend any sort of physical lure or appeal. For example, many of us love our friends, but there is nothing romantic about it. Personally, I love a good bacon cheeseburger. I can definitely promise you there is nothing romantic about that. Some people love their careers. Some love sports teams. Others love popular music groups. At the same time, people love their children, love their spouses, and love God. Hopefully there is a very different quality between the type of love a person has for a tasty burger and the type of love that same person has for his or her eternal companion.

I am grateful to one of my brothers, who taught me the value of expressing love for others. I have always loved my siblings but was never very good about telling this to them. Some years ago, my brother was going through a tough period in his life. He would often call and talk with me about his struggles. We would problem-solve and empathize together. We had wonderful conversations.

At the end of our phone calls, he started saying, "I love you." At first it caught me off guard, because we didn't really communicate this way. However, it was easy to respond in kind after he said it first. We ended our future conversations with similar expressions of love. I then found it easier and easier to end all such conversations with family members with "I love you," and they have done the same. It has been a true blessing to me, and I believe it has deepened the connections among us. There are no other people in the world I would rather be with than my family. I love them deeply. Expressing such feelings to them is important and has enriched my life.

Loving each other is sufficiently fundamental that we have actually been *commanded* to do it. Consider the short but impactful mortal ministry of our Savior Jesus Christ. He had only about three years to teach, by example and precept, how to return safely to our Heavenly Father. The night before His death, He met with His Apostles to give them His final instructions. After having given so much counsel and direction to them, He introduced in His last moments of mortality what He called a "new commandment." "A new commandment I give unto you, That ye love one another; as I have loved you, that ye also love one another" (John 13:34).

I have often considered why Jesus called this a *new* commandment. Surely the expectation to love each other had been present for generations. In fact, similar commands to love our neighbor date back from Christ's time more than a thousand years, to the time of Moses (see Leviticus 19:18). Yet Jesus said this was a new commandment. Under closer examination, truly this was a new commandment. It was not a commandment to simply love one another, but to love one another *as He had loved us.* Jesus had spent the prior three years demonstrating, modeling, and expressing His love for his brothers and sisters. Having provided a solid example of the behavior, He could now give the new commandment. He didn't want us to simply love one another; He wanted us to love one another with the same quality and intensity as *He* had shown. Such a commandment could only be given after the demonstration and example was provided.

As we reflect on the Savior's love for us, let's consider some of the characteristics of the love He personally demonstrated.

Godly love is primary. This means the Savior loved us first. He doesn't wait to love those who choose to love Him. He makes the initial step and extends His love to everyone. John, the beloved Apostle, rightly stated, "We love him, because he first loved us" (1 John 4:19). Reflecting on the example of my brother, I more easily said "I love you" to him after he first said it to me. By setting the example and loving us first, Jesus Christ opens the door for us to love Him and others.

Godly love is universal. The love of our Savior is identical to the love of our Heavenly Father, for they are alike in every way. We are all children of our Father in Heaven. He loves all of us. He does not discriminate based on gender, race, or any sort of individual difference. While He is able to give greater blessings to those who keep His commandments, He is able to love whomever He wants. God loves those who love Him. He is able to love those who do not love Him. He even offers His love to those who hate Him. He loves those who do not acknowledge Him and those who question whether He exists at all. As our Eternal Father, He extends His love and concern to all of His children and is constantly mindful of us.

Godly love is long-suffering. Our Savior loves us deeply, despite our flaws and shortcomings. His love continues even when we find it difficult to follow His commandments. He does not love us less when we fail. He loves us with a pure, perfect love. Because our feelings toward others often vary depending upon how they treat us, this aspect of godly love can be difficult to understand. As such, we don't really have a good frame of reference to understand someone who has the desire to love others *despite* their behavior. Nevertheless, it is true. God's love for us is long-suffering, and he is very patient with our weakness.

Having considered the qualities of God's love, consider now how *our* feelings of love often differ from those of God. Remember, loving others as God loves them is a *commandment*, and a very difficult one to fulfill. In some ways, it is one of the most difficult things we will do in life. It is a very advanced spiritual skill. Don't worry if you find your love for others does not match up to the way God loves them. You are in very good company with probably every other human being on the planet. Consider using the following questions to inspire personal areas of improvement to develop greater godlike love in your own life:

Is our love secondary? Do we wait for others to love us before we love them? Do we withhold affection until we stand to benefit from showing it? Loving others is a risky proposition, for it involves exposing ourselves to potential hurt. Many are afraid to take such risks and therefore remain guarded and keep their love safely inside. Expressing love requires an element of risk that can be difficult to accept.

The official handshake of the Boy Scouts of America is a traditional handshake, except done with the left hand. Although the origin of such a handshake is not truly known, the story goes that in the days of hand-to-hand combat with swords and shields, most warriors would use the sword with their right hand and hold the shield with their left. In order to shake hands with the right hand, the warrior would need to put his sword down but could keep his shield up. However, to shake hands with the left hand, the warrior had to *remove* his shield. Thus, it was a sign of trust to do a left-handed handshake and potentially leave oneself defenseless. At times, we may withhold our deepest love from others because we are afraid of getting hurt. We keep our emotional shields firmly in place and reach out cautiously with our other hand. However, we must put down our shields and reach out to others, regardless of whether they reach out to us, if we are to love as the Savior loves.

Is our love circumscribed? Do we try to love all groups of people, or are there certain groups we have difficulty loving? Is our decision to love someone limited by their age, socioeconomic status, education, nationality, or religious preference? Do we find ourselves easily accepting and loving people who are similar to us but passing hasty judgment on those who are different?

I served a full-time mission for The Church of Jesus Christ of Latter-day Saints in Mexico, which was my first exposure to a different culture. After spending only a few months in Mexico, I was astonished to discover that while the people looked a little different than I did and their language was much different than mine, we were alike in almost every other way. I remember meeting people that reminded me *exactly* of people I had known in the United States. I would realize, *Hey, that person is an exact Latino version of my good friend Jeff.* I quickly realized our differences were minimal and our similarities were vast. The more I came to know the people, the more I loved them. I still have great fondness for the people I knew while serving. They are some of the best people I have ever known. I truly believe we will find it is much easier to love those who are seemingly different from us if we avoid significant judgments based on a limited set of superficial characteristics and if we really try to get to know people before we make conclusions regarding the quality of their character.

Is our love too conditional? Do we withhold love from those who have wronged us? Do we have negative feelings toward those who are socially unacceptable? Unfortunately, it seems to be a base human tendency to harbor feelings of hatred at times. Hatred is such a damaging emotion, and it usually harms the person who feels it more than the object of his hatred. Nevertheless, as a society, we continue to find individuals or groups to hate. Sometimes these are large, faceless groups, such as hostile foreign nations or convicted criminals. Sometimes these are specific people who have hurt us in some way. In some cases, people feel absolutely justified in withholding love from those who have wronged them. They reason, *Why should I love that person when he clearly does not have my best interest in mind?* It is a compelling argument, strongly believed by many. However, the

Savior has given the exact opposite counsel. In the Sermon on the Mount, He instructed the people as follows: "Ye have heard that it hath been said, thou shalt love thy neighbor, and hate thine enemy. But I say unto you, love your enemies, bless them that curse you, do good to them that hate you, and pray for them which despitefully use you, and persecute you" (Matthew 5:43–44). Note how the Savior specifically mentions those who actively work against us. This isn't just the absentminded person who cuts us off while driving, but the person who saw us waiting for the parking space that was opening up and then intentionally hurried and took the spot. The Savior's direction is not only to love those who love us but also to love those who hate us. This is a tall order, but it is the essence of the love our Heavenly Father and Savior have for the entire human family.

I believe Jesus Christ's most magnificent characteristic is His capacity for love. I also believe His love for all His brothers and sisters was what motivated Him to be our Savior. It helped Him suffer the tremendous load of His Atonement. The condescension of God refers to the fact that Jesus Christ, the Creator of heaven and earth, agreed to lower Himself and become like those whom He created (see 1 Nephi 11:16–21). He chose to live among us instead of remaining in his heavenly home. He was exposed to the breadth of human emotions and challenges. He experienced hunger, thirst, disappointment, heartbreak, and every other difficulty we could possibly face. This is a manifestation of His love for us. He wanted to be among His brothers and sisters and show them the way back to heaven. He wanted to live by example and not just provide distant instruction from above. As the One charged with rescuing the children of Heavenly Father from death and sin, He literally provided a perfect path to follow by showing us the way.

Even though His mortal life was filled with challenges and difficulties, none of those experiences can compare with the suffering Jesus Christ experienced during His Atonement. Imagine a perfect being. A being with absolute insight who could understand the hearts and perceive the thoughts of those around Him. A being of incredible strength who perfectly resisted all temptations to the point of never being guilty of sin. Then, He enters the Garden of Gethsemane and takes on the burden of every misdeed, transgression, and sin that ever had been or ever would be committed. The Gospel of Mark describes Jesus as "sore amazed" at the experience (Mark 14:33). The omnipotent, omniscient Son of God was apparently *surprised* at how painful the process was. It was so painful that our dear Savior petitioned His Father in Heaven for relief. "And he said, Abba, Father, all things are possible unto thee; take away this cup from me: nevertheless not what I will, but what thou wilt" (Mark 14:36). It seems the Savior wanted to stop, at least at that time. He would later remark how part of Him desired to "shrink" and perhaps temporarily retreat from His responsibility to bear that tremendous load (see Doctrine and Covenants 19:18). What sustained Him through this great difficulty? Why did He continue despite every fiber of His eternal being screaming out in physical, emotional, and spiritual agony?

He continued because He loves us. No sense of duty could have overcome the strain. No feeling of obligation or requirement could have helped Him push past the difficulty. It was His absolute love for each of His brothers and sisters that provided the strength. I like to believe, in that moment of incomprehensible grief, He thought about us. Perhaps He thought of us individually. *How can I quit now? Jason will never have a chance to make it back to Father. I love Jason; I have to continue for him.* As an angel came to strengthen the Savior during this time, I like to believe they talked about us. "And what about Jamie? And Daphne? And John and Frank? What will they do without your help?" Scripture does not record detailed insight into the Savior's thoughts and feelings during this time. I believe He thought to Himself, *I'll do it for them. I love them. I'll do anything I have to in order for them to be happy and come back to the presence of our Father in Heaven.*

So, the Savior continued. He bled from every pore. He subjected Himself to the cruel process of scourging. He bore the heavy beam that would ultimately bear Him. He endured the merciless torture of crucifixion, amidst the jeers and taunts of those He loved and was dying to save. Even while hanging in that agonizing position, He gave comfort to one of the thieves being executed beside Him and pled for forgiveness for His torturers (see Luke 23:33–43). *This* is the quality of the love Jesus Christ has for us. When Nephi talked about being "filled with *his* love," he was referring to this. This is the type of love we are commanded to have for one another. It is a significant requirement indeed!

What can we do to develop this amazing love? There are several steps to accomplish this. First, we can pray for it. When referring to charity, the pure love of Christ, the Book of Mormon prophet Mormon directed as follows: "Wherefore, my beloved brethren, pray unto the Father with all the energy of heart, that ye may be filled with this love, which he hath bestowed upon all who are true followers of his Son, Jesus Christ" (Moroni 7:48). First, we can ask God to fill us with the type of love that Jesus has for us. We should ask sincerely and be ready for the process that will likely follow. As some of you may have experienced in your lives, asking Heavenly Father for such things as patience, love, or humility usually results in opportunities that will help develop such characteristics. Learning to develop love like the type God has for us will follow a similar pattern.

Second, we need to make room for such love in our hearts. This means our hearts cannot be filled with anger, hatred, or intolerance toward others. God will not forcibly remove such feelings to replace them with loving ones, especially if we continue to harbor such feelings. He respects our agency and will permit us to keep those emotions and attitudes if we desire. If you are on your knees praying to Father in Heaven to be filled with the love of God toward someone or something you actively and intentionally hate, settle in for a long wait. You will have to rid yourself of angry feelings first so God can replace them with loving ones.

In the allegory of the tame and wild olive trees found in the fifth chapter of Jacob, the Lord of the vineyard gives direction to the servant regarding how to nurture the trees. There were many trees that had produced bad branches and bad fruit. The servants were removing the bad branches and replacing them with good ones. Consider the direction they were given:

> Wherefore ye shall clear away the bad according as the good shall grow, that the root and the top may be equal in strength, until the good shall overcome the bad, and the bad be hewn down and cast into the fire, that they cumber not the ground of my vineyard; and thus will I sweep away the bad out of my vineyard. (Jacob 5:66)

The servants were directed to only remove the bad as the good grew in strength and might. Such it is with our lives. The bad can be removed only as we seek to replace it with good. You will develop a greater capacity for love as you eliminate feelings of hate and anger.

Finally, welcome the opportunities that will present themselves for you to develop the type of love the Savior has for us. Our Heavenly Father allows us to work and struggle to develop celestial characteristics. This seems to be the best way for us to become like Him. For example, I remember wanting a portable music player as a teenager. I approached my father with the request, and he agreed it was a reasonable purchase for a young man. We went together to a local electronics store and perused the many available options. As we went our separate ways to explore, I found an excellent model. It was sleek, compact, and had multiple advanced functions. It was one of the higher-end models and somewhat expensive. My father and I met in the store, and he asked me if I had found something I liked. I told him I had and showed him the unit. He remarked how it was a great item and then wanted to show me something he had found. We walked to the area where the less-expensive models were, and he pointed out a very reasonably priced device. It was larger, bulkier, and less sophisticated than the one I wanted. It was also about half the price.

My dad asked me which one I wanted more, and I responded how I preferred the more expensive model. He then said, "Okay. If you want a portable music player today, I will buy the less expensive one for you right now. However, if you want the more expensive model, you'll have to save money for it. I'll put up half the cost, but you'll have to come up with the rest. What would you like to do?" Resisting my impulse for immediate gratification, I chose to wait and save money for the more expensive item. It took several months of work. Eventually I was able to save sufficient funds and make the purchase. What followed was the most interesting part of all: I took exceptional care of that music player! I put it away carefully after every use. I cleaned it regularly. As a result, it remained in good functioning condition for several years. I am convinced the reason I took such great care was because I knew the value of the purchase. I had worked hard and remembered the time and effort invested in order to obtain it.

In His wisdom, this is one of the reasons Heavenly Father gives us opportunities to develop good characteristics. If you want to develop the love of Christ in your heart and go through the trials and sacrifices to get there, you will be much more likely to treasure the newfound ability you have achieved. In addition, as you go through the process, you will learn other skills that you can use to bless your own life and the lives of those around you. Your Father in Heaven will present you with chances to grow and change as you strive to develop the love of God in your heart. Welcome these opportunities and try to recognize them for the good things they are. Although they may look like trials and challenges at the outset, they will eventually bless your life.

Being filled with the love of God will not only help us love others better but will also help us love ourselves better. As our hearts begin to fill with His love, feelings of self-doubt will fade. Not only will we develop greater faith and trust in others, but we will also develop greater faith and trust in ourselves. We will be less likely to judge and more eager to forgive, *both others and ourselves.* President Dieter F. Uchtdorf of the First Presidency explained the following:

> You are loved. You are dear to your heavenly parents. The infinite and eternal Creator of light and life knows you! He is mindful of you. Yes, God loves you this very day and always. He is not waiting to love you until you have overcome your weaknesses and bad habits. He loves you today with a full

understanding of your struggles. He is aware that you reach up to Him in heartfelt and hopeful prayer. He knows of the times you have held onto the fading light and believed—even in the midst of growing darkness. He knows of your sufferings. He knows of your remorse for the times you have fallen short or failed. And still He loves you.[4]

Developing this kind of love for ourselves and others will increase our spiritual strength. It will help us cope more effectively with trials and challenges. The sacrifices we make in order to develop Christlike love will yield blessings in the end.

Key Concept 2
Make any necessary changes to learn how to love others as the Savior loves us.

QUESTIONS FOR SELF-REFLECTION
- Am I comfortable saying "I love you" to those I am closest to? If not, what can I do to change that?
- How do I feel when I consider the Savior's love for me?
- How do I believe the Savior feels about me personally?
- What can I change in order to have greater feelings of love for people in general?

---

4   Dieter F. Uchtdorf, "Living the Gospel Joyful," *Ensign*, Nov. 2014, 123.

CHAPTER 5
"Behold, He Hath Heard My Cry"

Why does Heavenly Father ask us to pray to Him?
What are the purposes of prayer?

IN THE MIDST OF HIS grief, Nephi was reminded of the many times he had communicated with Heavenly Father and how his prayers had been answered. He stated, "Behold, he hath heard my cry by day, and he hath given me knowledge by visions in the night-time. And by day have I waxed bold in mighty prayer before him; yea, my voice have I sent up on high; and angels came down and ministered unto me" (2 Nephi 4:23–24). Nephi recognized the incredible privilege of prayer. He used this privilege to cope with his struggles and gain insight into the reasons for his suffering.

What a blessing it is to be able to communicate with the Creator of the universe with a single thought or audible word! This blessing is even more spectacular when we consider also the fact that He is always listening and eager to respond. Our Father in Heaven longs to hear from us, and He absolutely blesses those who reach out to Him in sincerity and humility. One of my favorite hymns teaches the following about the power of prayer: "Oh, how praying rests the weary! Prayer will change the night to day."[5] I have found that statement to be true at many times in my life.

Years ago, a friend told me he didn't think he needed to pray. He stated Heavenly Father knows our thoughts anyway and therefore telling them to Him is redundant. I recall thinking he was probably wrong about the need for prayer but didn't necessarily disagree with his logic. I later learned there is much more to prayer than just communicating our thoughts to Father in Heaven. Prayer is a process that trains us in humility and accountability as well.

When Adam and Eve were in the Garden of Eden, they both transgressed a commandment. They partook of the forbidden fruit after having received

---

5   "Did You Think to Pray?" *Hymns,* no. 140.

strict direction not to do so. Upon discovering they were naked, they heard the voice of the Lord as they walked in the garden. Anticipating His arrival and not wanting to be found naked and disobedient, Adam and Eve hid themselves from the Lord. As God arrived in the garden, He simply asked, "Adam, where art thou?" (Genesis 3:9).

I have always thought that was a curious question for the Lord to ask. He is omniscient. He sees everything we do. Not only did He *know* where Adam was, but He had also *watched* the whole drama play out from the moment Eve was tempted by Lucifer. Nevertheless, God asked Adam to reveal himself. Once Adam did this and admitted the reason for hiding was because he was naked, the Lord asked again, "Who told thee that thou wast naked? Hast thou eaten of the tree, whereof I commanded thee that thou shouldest not eat?" (Genesis 3:11). Again, this seems like a strange question from an all-knowing being. He knew *exactly* who had told Adam he was naked and knew precisely how Adam had partaken of the forbidden fruit. Yet He asked these questions of Adam for some reason.

It does not appear the Lord was trying to gather historical information from Adam. However, He *was* trying to gather a different type of information. It seems He wanted to know if Adam would be accountable for his transgression. He wanted Adam to be responsible and confess what had happened. Adam did confess, consistent with his honest character. This is one of the purposes of prayer and what my friend, who thought praying was redundant, did not understand. We don't pray to God because *He* needs to know things about our life. We pray to God to tell Him about what *we* have done, how *we* feel, and what *we* desire of Him. We humble ourselves and make requests in faith. The act of prayer increases spiritual strength. It builds meekness. It helps us appreciate our true position before God. It teaches us we are absolutely dependent upon His mercy and grace for everything we have and need.

We are commanded to pray, just as we are commanded to love one another. Indeed, we are commanded to pray *always*. "Verily, verily, I say unto you, ye must watch and pray always, lest ye be tempted by the devil, and ye be led away captive by him" (3 Nephi 18:15). There are many similar commands in ancient and modern scripture to "pray always" (see Doctrine and Covenants 10:5; Luke 21:36; 2 Nephi 32:9; Doctrine and Covenants 33:17; Ephesians 6:18; Doctrine and Covenants 93:49) and countless more admonitions to pray. Some of the promised blessings from praying include protection from temptation, blessings to our spouses and families, forgiveness of sins, and having the Lord's Spirit poured out upon us. Whereas our Father in Heaven desires to bless us with all manner of wonderful things, He waits until we exercise obedience and faith before doing so. This is essential for our spiritual growth. As part of preparation to receive such blessings, He commands we ask for them first.

What does it mean to pray *always*? While the commandment does not require us to be on our knees in continuous formal prayer, it does invite us to keep an open channel of communication with God. An event from the life of Nephi provides a good example to understand what it means to pray always.

Nephi and his brothers were commanded to return to Jerusalem to retrieve the plates of brass from Laban, which contained the scriptures and their genealogy. Their first plan was to simply have Laman ask Laban to give them the record. That plan didn't work. Laban cast Laman out and threatened to kill him. Their second plan was to essentially bribe Laban with their considerable riches. Laban rejected that offer as well and cast them out while keeping their precious things. The group of brothers was clearly discouraged, and Laman and Lemuel were about to leave without having accomplished the task. Nephi had already sworn an oath to do what they had been commanded to do (see 1 Nephi 3:15), and he relied upon the whisperings of the Spirit to know what course to follow. He went back himself to try to obtain the plates of brass. As he approached the house of Laban, he found Laban drunk and unconscious on the ground. Nephi then had an interaction with the Spirit that goes somewhat as follows:

Spirit: Nephi, you must kill Laban.

Nephi: I've never killed anyone. It's against the commandments. I really don't want to do it.

Spirit: God has put Laban into this position so you can accomplish what you have been commanded to do.

Nephi: Well, he did try to kill us, and he stole all of our things as well . . .

Spirit: You must kill him. The Lord has delivered him unto you for this purpose. The Lord removes the wicked so that His righteousness can be accomplished. It is better for one wicked person to die than for a whole nation to be led astray and ultimately perish.

Nephi: I know we have been promised to be blessed if we keep the commandments. We can't keep the commandments very well if we don't have them to refer to. The commandments are recorded on the plates of brass. This is why Laban is lying drunk before me. If I am obedient to God and slay him, then I can obtain the record and give my people a chance to keep the commandments and be blessed (see 1 Nephi 4:7–18).

In this situation, Nephi is communicating with God and essentially praying. However, I'm fairly confident he wasn't on his knees with his eyes closed, arms folded, saying a vocal prayer. In fact, he was an intruder near the house of a man whose servants would likely kill Nephi on sight. He was probably on high alert and taking evasive action. Nevertheless, he was communicating with God in his thoughts while going about the necessary business of his mission. I think this is a good example of "praying always." We need to constantly have our Father in Heaven in the back of our minds. Naturally, there are many things we must do throughout the day, which require significant attention and focus. The things of heaven are not going to be at the front of our minds during such times, nor do they need to be. However, they should always be present in our thoughts as a backdrop, guiding our daily lives. We can make better choices and avoid temptation if we remember Heavenly Father in all that we do.

While we should pray always in this fashion, we also need to make sure we have formal prayers on a daily basis. This type of prayer needs to be more deliberate. Ideally, it should involve a quiet place and a proper frame of mind. Preparing ourselves to pray is almost as important as the act of prayer itself. Many of you have probably given a talk in sacrament meeting. In anticipation of this, you likely researched your topic, prepared an outline, and carefully considered what you would say to the congregation. You may have even gone through several drafts before finally arriving at the final version of your talk. Those who have gone through such preparation have probably given a good discourse, enjoyed by those who received it. Do we employ such preparation before we pray? Do we give careful thought beforehand to what we want to say to our Father in Heaven? Do we research the recent events in our life to see what is most important to discuss with Him? This is not to suggest that each of our prayers needs to be like a formal talk. But if we spend a good amount of time preparing to speak to fellow members of the Church, perhaps we should give more than casual consideration as we prepare to speak to our Heavenly Father. More intentional preparation before we pray will improve the quality and sincerity of our prayers.

We should pray individually and privately to our Father in Heaven. Private prayer, done once or more per day, can help us stay close to the Spirit. This is our chance to communicate directly with God and improve our relationship with Him. If we are married, we should pray together with our spouse. This is a wonderful opportunity to develop greater emotional intimacy and marital harmony. If we have children, we should pray together with them. This sets a fine example of humility and the importance of prayer. It will also strengthen our families and increase family unity.

Prayer is a personal and intimate experience and should be done with sincerity. Jesus taught,

> And when thou prayest, thou shalt not be as the hypocrites are: for they love to pray standing in the synagogues and in the corners of the streets, that they may be seen of men. Verily I say unto you, They have their reward. But thou, when thou prayest, enter into thy closet, and when thou hast shut thy door, pray to thy Father which is in secret; and thy Father which seeth in secret shall reward thee openly. But when ye pray, use not vain repetitions, as the heathen do: for they think that they shall be heard for their much speaking. (Matthew 6:5–7)

Consider the phrase, "vain repetitions." Sometimes we find ourselves praying for the same things over and over again. We pray for our safety, for the safety of our spouses and children, for our health, for our friends and loved ones, and so on. If we pray for these things over and over, is this a vain repetition? I believe it depends upon our attitude. *What* we say in our prayers is probably not nearly as important as the level of our sincerity during prayer. Our Father in Heaven knows whether we are sincere or not, yet we should make sure our prayers are heartfelt, genuine, and honest.

Alma's Book of Mormon account of the apostate Zoramites contains a clear example of vain repetition. These people had fallen away from the true gospel but continued to worship God in a perverted manner. They had built churches and gathered there one day a week to pray. However, their prayers were proud and insincere. In fact, they had developed a single prayer that was read by each person in the congregation, one at a time, in succession. The prayer essentially proclaimed them better than everyone else, denied the true nature of God, and claimed there would be no Christ (see Alma 31:15–18). Mormon makes the following observation regarding this unorthodox practice:

> Now, from this stand they did offer up, every man, the selfsame prayer unto God, thanking their God that they were chosen of him, and that he did not lead them away after the tradition of their brethren, and that their hearts were not stolen away to believe in things to come, which they knew nothing about. Now, after the people had all offered up thanks after this manner, they returned to their homes, *never speaking of their*

God again until they had assembled themselves together again to the holy stand, to offer up thanks after their manner. (Alma 31:22–23; emphasis added)

Although these people were technically praying, their hearts were far from God. Repeating a rehearsed script once a week in church and then not even mentioning the name of God during the rest of the week is a classic example of a vain repetition. Do not worry if you find yourself honestly praying for the same things over and over again. However, if our prayers lack sincerity, we are unlikely to gain the spiritual strength that prayer can yield. As previously mentioned, preparing ourselves to pray can guard against casual or insincere communication with God.

What should we pray about? What should we pray for? The answer is "anything and everything." If it is genuinely important to you, it is likely important to your Father in Heaven as well. Sometimes we think, *This is such a trivial matter; why would Heavenly Father be interested in this?* Yet the opposite is true. I remember when one of our children was little. He had a treasured action figure that he played with each day. One day he had misplaced his toy. We couldn't find it, despite all our efforts. The poor boy was distraught with anguish. He suggested we pray to locate the toy.

Pray about a toy? *Really?* It seemed so inconsequential! Surely God has better things to do with His time in a world where wars rage and Satan's power increases daily. But that is the misconception. Our Father in Heaven *doesn't* have higher priorities than the care and nurture of His children (see Moses 1:39). My son and I knelt in prayer, asked Heavenly Father to help us find the toy, and then looked again. We found it. That toy has long since been discarded, but the lesson regarding prayer remains.

Remember, your Heavenly Father loves you with a deep and incredible love. I imagine He is thrilled when you take the time to tell Him about your life, even the most mundane details. Surely He relishes that quiet time between the two of you. I am confident He looks forward to those special moments. Perhaps He is a little saddened when we either forget to pray or spend so little time and energy in our prayers that the communication is nonexistent. Amulek, a Book of Mormon prophet, gave excellent counsel regarding what we can pray for:

Cry unto him when ye are in your fields, yea, over all your flocks. Cry unto him in your houses, yea, over all your household, both morning, mid-day, and evening. Yea, cry unto him against the power of your enemies. Yea, cry unto him against the devil, who is an enemy to all righteousness. Cry unto him over the crops of your fields, that ye may prosper in them. Cry over the flocks of your fields, that they may increase. But this is not all; ye must pour out your souls in your closets, and your secret places, and in your wilderness. Yea, and when you do not cry unto the Lord, let your hearts be full, drawn out in prayer unto him continually for your welfare, and also for the welfare of those who are around you. (Alma 34:20–27)

Amulek suggests we pray unto the Lord regarding our livelihoods, our families, and our employment; that we pray against the power of the devil; and that we pray for those around us as well. It is just as important for us to thank God for what we have been given as it is to ask God for those things we need. Gratitude is essential in developing spiritual strength. We are unlikely to achieve greater spiritual potential without first acknowledging how we have been blessed in the first place. Any casual analysis of our lives will reveal a multitude of blessings from God. A *careful* analysis of our lives will likely reveal more blessings than we can possibly count. If you consider the oxygen you just breathed in, which was used to refresh your blood, which powered your brain, which controlled your eyeballs, which were used to read this last sentence—all of which you did absolutely nothing to merit—you'll start to understand how deep our gratitude can become. We have so many things to be thankful for, regardless of our situation. We need to ensure our prayers are full of gratitude. In fact, that is a commandment as well. "Thou shalt thank the Lord thy God in all things" (D&C 59:7).

Prayer will increase the quality of our relationship with Heavenly Father, just as regular and sincere communication with another human being will improve a relationship. The more we talk to God about our trials, successes, challenges, and joys, the more we will understand His will for us. Remember, we enjoyed a very close relationship with Him before we came to this earth. Prayer becomes part of recalling and rekindling that relationship in mortality. In fact, it would seem our very salvation is at least partially dependent on developing a relationship with God. Jesus stated, "And this is life eternal, that they might *know thee* the only true God, and Jesus Christ, whom thou hast sent" (John 17:3; emphasis added).

It seems logical Satan would encourage us not to pray since he is intent on our destruction and misery. "For the evil spirit teacheth not a man to pray, but teacheth him that he must not pray" (2 Nephi 32:8). He does not want us to improve our relationship with Heavenly Father. Every step we take closer to God is a step we take further from Lucifer. The battle for our souls is in full effect, and prayer is one of the simplest tools to defeat Satan. We are easily led to believe it is not necessary *because* it is so simple. Perhaps you have heard Satan whisper these lies to you in the past:

"You don't have time to pray; just do it later."

"Missing one prayer isn't going to matter that much."

"You are not worthy to pray, considering what you've just done."

Prayer appears to be a serious threat to Satan's agenda, judging by the amount of force he employs to derail it. If it were as insignificant as he suggests it is, then why does he fight so much against it? He *knows* it is powerful and tempts us to resist, delay, or refuse to engage in this behavior. Brigham Young stated the following regarding our need to pray: "It matters not whether you or I feel like praying, when the time comes to pray, pray. If we do not feel like it, we should pray till we do. . . . You will find that those who wait till the Spirit bids them pray, will never pray much on this earth."[6]

Make prayer a priority in your life. Praying often will provide refuge from the storms that gather around you. Praying sincerely and honestly will provide the peace the Savior has promised to His followers. Elder Richard G. Scott of the Quorum of the Twelve Apostles gave the following wise counsel and promise:

> Choose to converse with your Father in Heaven often. Make time every day to share your thoughts and feelings with Him. Tell Him everything that concerns you. He is interested in the most important as well as the most mundane facets of your life. Share with Him your full range of feelings and experiences. Because He respects your agency, Father in Heaven will never force you to pray to Him. But as you exercise that agency and include Him in every aspect of your daily life, your heart will begin to fill with peace, buoyant peace. That peace will focus an eternal light on your struggles. It will help you to manage those challenges from an eternal perspective.[7]

You will increase your ability to manage difficult times and build your relationship with Heavenly Father as you create a diligent habit of prayer. Your resilience and sense of peace will increase. Once again, the familiar hymn teaches truth and reminds us of the power that comes through earnest communication

---

6   Brigham Young, *Discourses of Brigham Young*, sel. John A. Widtsoe (1926), 68.

7   Richard G. Scott, "Make the Exercise of Faith Your First Priority," *Ensign*, Nov. 2014, 93.

with God: "Oh, how praying rests the weary! Prayer will change the night to day. So, when life gets dark and dreary, don't forget to pray."[8]

Key Concept 3

Develop a consistent pattern of meaningful, sincere, and frequent prayer.

QUESTIONS FOR SELF-REFLECTION

* What can I do to make my prayers more sincere?
* Do I ever find myself too busy to pray? If so, what can I do to make time to pray regularly?
* What sorts of things do I typically pray about?
* How can I improve my relationship with Heavenly Father through prayer?

---

8   "Did You Think to Pray?" *Hymns,* no. 140.

CHAPTER 6
"Do Not Anger Again Because of Mine Enemies"

Why is forgiveness necessary?
Why are we required to forgive all people?

PREVIOUS CHAPTERS HAVE REFERRED TO things we *should* do in order to build greater spiritual resilience. Our loving Father in Heaven provides many recommendations and suggestions of things we can add to our lives so He can bless us more abundantly. There are also things He commands we should *not* do—things to avoid so we can spare ourselves unnecessary grief. Nephi's consideration of his life and behavior reminded him of a very important strategy as he stated, "Do not anger again because of mine enemies. Do not slacken my strength because of mine afflictions" (2 Nephi 4:29). Nephi understood how managing his anger and forgiving others would increase his personal peace and help him cope more effectively. This concept is highly applicable to all of us, since we all have at least one common enemy in Lucifer and have all suffered afflictions.

Nephi had much experience with both spiritual and physical "enemies." Two of his older brothers were jealous of and hostile toward him from the time he was young. They attempted to murder him or leave him for dead on multiple occasions. After they made the journey from the desert to Jerusalem to retrieve the plates of brass, Lehi asked them to perform this dangerous sojourn once again. This time the purpose was to convince Ishmael and his family to leave their homes and travel to the promised land with them. Laman and Lemuel did not seem to complain this time, as one of the purposes in recruiting Ishmael's family was to provide prospective spouses for Lehi's children. Although the brothers successfully persuaded Ishmael's family to travel to the wilderness, problems soon arose on the return journey.

Laman and Lemuel, now with fresh support from several of the children of Ishmael, decided they did not want to travel back to the desert camp of

Lehi. They wanted to return to Jerusalem. Knowing this could result in serious consequences for all involved, Nephi spoke firmly and directly to his brothers to convince them to abandon their plans. Laman and Lemuel became enraged at being rebuked by their younger brother. In their fierce anger, they bound Nephi and left him in the wilderness to die (see 1 Nephi 7:1–16). Nephi sought heavenly help in this desperate situation.

> But it came to pass that I prayed unto the Lord, saying: O Lord, according to my faith which is in thee, wilt thou deliver me from the hands of my brethren; yea, even give me strength that I may burst these bands with which I am bound. And it came to pass that when I had said these words, behold, the bands were loosed from off my hands and feet, and I stood before my brethren, and I spake unto them again. (1 Nephi 7:17–18)

Nephi was miraculously delivered from what would have been certain death. Even after this event, his brothers tried to attack him again. Two of Ishmael's children and Ishmael's wife intervened and begged Laman and Lemuel to stop. Laman and Lemuel were struck with a burst of uncharacteristic contrition. Not only did they cease their murderous intentions, but they also pled with Nephi for forgiveness (see 1 Nephi 7:19–20).

This presented an interesting situation for Nephi. Should he forgive his brothers? Should he hold on to what he could have considered "justified anger" at their actions? Consider the reasoning Nephi might have gone through as he pondered his options.

Reasons for Nephi to withhold forgiveness from his brothers:
- Laman and Lemuel made repeated attempts to harm Nephi.
- His brothers' wicked behavior was chronic, willful, and malicious.
- Efforts to rehabilitate them had been largely fruitless.
- Their "contrition" seemed to be motivated by social pressures and not by a genuine desire for change.
- If the situation were reversed and Nephi had somehow wronged them, they would likely withhold forgiveness from him (possibly indefinitely).

Some of these justifications are more reasonable than others, but all of them come from Nephi's constant enemy: Satan. Whereas Jesus Christ is the Prince of Peace, Satan is the father of contention. He did not want Nephi to forgive *or* forget. He would rather Nephi have kept the wound fresh for years and become angry because of his enemies. Now contemplate the rationale on the opposite side of the argument of whether or not to forgive.

Reasons for Nephi to forgive his brothers:
- Our Father in Heaven has asked us to forgive one another.
- Nephi's lack of forgiveness would hurt only himself.
- Forgiving is the Christlike thing to do.

The first of these reasons is the most important. Faithful followers of Christ will strive to keep His commandments, regardless of their own personal issues. Nephi did not hesitate to do as the Lord instructs. After his brothers asked him for forgiveness, he responded, "And it came to pass that I did frankly forgive them all that they had done, and I did exhort them that they would pray unto the Lord their God for forgiveness" (1 Nephi 7:21).

What a wonderful yet terribly difficult example to emulate! Many of us have been wronged at some point in our lives. In the majority of those cases, the offending party was probably unaware of the misdeed and meant no harm. In some of the cases, the offending party may have been unaware of the misdeed but behaved insensitively or selfishly. In rare cases, the offending party had malicious intent and deliberately tried to create difficulty and sorrow in our lives. Those who are the victims of such behavior suffer innocently. One could easily justify that forgiveness would not be advisable in such a situation. Why should one forgive another who has spitefully inflicted pain?

In contrast to popular opinion, the Lord gives direction regarding how to handle such situations:

> My disciples, in days of old, sought occasion against one another and forgave not one another in their hearts; and for this evil they were afflicted and sorely chastened. Wherefore, I say unto you, that ye ought to forgive one another; for he that forgiveth not his brother his trespasses standeth condemned before the Lord; for there remaineth in him the greater sin. I, the Lord, will forgive whom I will forgive, *but of you it is required to forgive all men.* (D&C 64:8–10; emphasis added)

This is a very interesting doctrine. Essentially, it states that the sin of withholding forgiveness is much worse than it might seem on the surface. Many people wouldn't even consider the withholding of forgiveness to be sinful at all. Sometimes we feel justified in such behavior because of the wrongs that have been done to us. Yet this scripture indicates we must forgive *all* people. If we do not, there remains in us the greater sin.

Apply this doctrine to Nephi's situation. Nephi was yelled at, beaten, tied up, and left for dead. Yet if he did not forgive his brothers, then Nephi himself would be *more guilty* than they. That can be a difficult reality to accept, yet the doctrine is clear. We are required to forgive everyone.

Why does the Lord ask us to forgive? Why does He require us to let go of our anger? Why does He ask us to move past situations in which we have been deliberately wronged? Such forgiveness is not common behavior in most people. We often want justice when someone has trespassed against us. We want them to pay for their misdeeds. We may believe that if we were to forgive them, then somehow they are no longer accountable for their sinful acts. However, holding on to grudges and refusing to forgive is usually much more punishing to oneself than it is to the offender.

In states where the death penalty is legal, there are often observation rooms where relatives of victims can come to witness the execution. This is apparently designed to provide a measure of comfort to them. It is meant to be a final recompense for the injustices they suffered. In many cases, the victims have lost a loved one due to criminal behavior. Usually years and even decades have passed since the crime was committed due to the many appeals and legal circumstances associated with the death penalty. The families of victims assemble to witness the final act of justice. They have waited for so long to finally feel better, and they long for the relief they have sought for so many years. They believe they can finally rest once the perpetrator is dead. However, in many documented accounts of such events, the families report there was no sense of relief. In the case of lethal injection, some have commented how the perpetrator seemed to die so peacefully. "It isn't fair!" they seem to cry. "He needs to suffer like my brother suffered when he was killed. He needs to suffer like I have suffered for these fourteen years living with the grief of having lost my closest friend." They all inevitably leave the execution chamber still filled with sorrow and having lost their last apparent recourse to fill their emptiness. The event they had anticipated for so long has come and gone, and they are no closer to happiness than they were before.

Gary Ridgway, otherwise known as the Green River Killer, was convicted on December 18, 2003, of forty-eight counts of first-degree murder. The families of the victims were permitted to confront Mr. Ridgway at the sentencing. Family after family came forward, accusing the killer of being a horrible person. They remarked how they hoped he would suffer the rest of his days. Eventually, it was Robert Rule's turn. His sixteen-year-old daughter was one of the victims. Mr.

Rule made the following statement: "Mr. Ridgway, there are people here who hate you. I'm not one of them. I forgive you for what you have done. You've made it difficult to live up to what I believe, and what God says to do, and that is to forgive. And he doesn't say to forgive certain people, he says to forgive all. So you are forgiven, sir."[9]

Those who witnessed the event said Mr. Rule's statement brought Mr. Ridgway to tears. It was particularly poignant considering that observers noted that the defendant had shown no emotion through all the other statements and accusations.

This account highlights one of the main reasons God asks us to forgive all people. Forgiveness is not for the benefit of the offending party. *Forgiveness is for our benefit.* As we hold on to old hurts and long-standing grudges, the only person we really damage is ourselves. A popular saying of unknown origin goes somewhat as follows: Bearing a grudge or refusing to forgive is like drinking poison and then hoping your neighbor will feel ill. Hate and anger are destructive to the soul. The *reasons* we feel hate or anger are inconsequential. Comparing again to poison, where the poison came from doesn't matter. It is still sickening. It makes no difference *why* we resist forgiveness or whether or not we feel justified in this behavior. The longer we resist forgiving others, the longer we will continue to experience the negative consequences.

Sometimes we refuse to forgive because we want the offending party to truly feel how much they have hurt us. We want them to somehow pay for their actions. Forgiving other people does not absolve them of their misdeeds. Every person has to be accountable for his or her own actions. Our forgiveness has nothing to do with *their* standing before God. It has no bearing on the final state of their soul. However, our forgiveness has *plenty* to do with our standing before God and the final state of our souls. God is our judge and will exercise perfect justice and mercy toward all of us. We don't need to mete out judgment. In fact, we are specifically commanded not to (see Matthew 7:1–2). As we truly forgive those who have hurt us, regardless of whether or not we feel they deserve forgiveness, we free our souls and increase our spiritual power and personal peace.

God gave us the tremendous gift of agency, which includes the ability to choose between good and evil. This means we have the power to exercise control of our emotions and how we feel about other people. We give up some of that power when we allow the actions of others to dictate our emotional responses. People will anger or upset us, but we determine our response. Being a slave to

9   Elaine Porterfield, "Green River Victim's Family Finds Peace in Forgiveness," *Seattle Post-Intelligencer Reporter,* Dec. 19, 2003, accessed Jul. 7, 2015, http://www.seattlepi.com/local/article/Green-River-victim-s-family-finds-peace-in-1132659.php.

our emotional reactions is a frustrating position to be in. The Atonement of Jesus Christ is the means to serious and lasting change.

One of Satan's strategies is to try to convince us we cannot change. He preaches we are born with certain character flaws and that's "just the way we are." Such philosophies prevent us from necessary change and growth. One of the challenges of life is that we naturally come with certain flaws and weaknesses. A loving Father in Heaven permits these to remain so we can grow and progress. Just because a habit or behavior seems to be very natural and part of our character does not mean it will forever be a part of who we are. Yet as people try to change long-standing habits, they often find the process is difficult. They find chronic behavior is resistant to modification. They mistakenly conclude, "That's just the way I am; I cannot change." Lehi the prophet warned his rebellious sons about the danger of being burdened with sinful behavior: "O that ye would awake; awake from a deep sleep, yea, even from the sleep of hell, and shake off the awful chains by which ye are bound, which are the chains which bind the children of men, that they are carried away captive down to the eternal gulf of misery and woe" (2 Nephi 1:13).

By liberating ourselves from the chains of withholding forgiveness, harboring anger, or indulging in sinful behavior, we will truly gain greater confidence before God. We will experience an increase in happiness in this life. Whatever our Heavenly Father commands us to do will ultimately bring us joy and peace. He loves us very much and does everything He can to help us navigate this life with happiness.

In addition to avoiding personal damage, by forgiving others we also achieve spiritual growth. This earth life is a time for us to become like our Father in Heaven. We are here to begin the development of the characteristics and qualities He possesses. We develop such characteristics the same way we develop any other talent or skill. If we desired to become proficient at tennis, for example, we would expect long hours of practice, study, and sacrifice to improve our abilities. If we never practiced or if we disregarded the advice of our coach, we likely wouldn't see any improvement. It is no different with spiritual development. We must practice those celestial qualities that God possesses if we are to eventually become like Him.

Elder Dallin H. Oaks of the Quorum of the Twelve Apostles relayed a modern-day parable, which explains this concept very succinctly:

> A wealthy father knew that if he were to bestow his wealth upon a child who had not yet developed the needed wisdom and stature, the inheritance would probably be wasted. The father said

to his child: "All that I have I desire to give you—not only my wealth, but also my position and standing among men. That which I *have* I can easily give you, but that which I *am* you must obtain for yourself. You will qualify for your inheritance by learning what I have learned and by living as I have lived. I will give you the laws and principles by which I have acquired my wisdom and stature. Follow my example, mastering as I have mastered, and you will become as I am, and all that I have will be yours.[10]

Our Father in Heaven is a very, *very* forgiving individual. We come to Him again and again with problems, missteps, and sins. He consistently forgives and welcomes us back. His loving kindness is extended to both the naive who make simple mistakes and the deliberately rebellious who sin as if they have impunity. If we are going to become like our Father in Heaven, doesn't it make sense that we need to "practice" forgiving others now? How can we expect to become a compassionate, forgiving being if we consistently withhold forgiveness and harbor resentment? Learning to forgive not only brings us satisfaction and peace in this life but also helps prepare us for the eternal life we will live after our mortality is over.

When my wife and I were newlyweds, we were poor college students with big hopes and dreams. Yet, like mostly newlyweds, our situation was bleak. We lived in the basement of a home that should have been condemned, school was difficult, and money was tight. One day I received a Publishers Clearing House envelope in the mail that said, "David Morgan, you may have won a million dollars!" Normally I would have tossed it in the trash, remembering from my youth that my parents received such mail, and it was obviously a mass mailing. I knew those letters addressed to my parents were mass mailings and not winning certificates because of the way they were printed. The bulk of the "winning letter" was printed in one font, while my mom or dad's name was printed in a clearly different font. That was a dead giveaway that they hadn't been selected for the grand prize. However, the letter that came to me this time was different. The font to print my name and the font to print the rest of the letter were the same. I figured the creators of the letter would not have gone to the trouble of printing such a letter if it were not the true winner. I held the letter in my trembling hands. "It is happening. We've won a million dollars. I mean, how could it be fake? Look at the font! It's the same for the whole letter!" For the next few hours, I mentally spent that million dollars. I would become one of

10 Dallin H. Oaks, "The Challenge to Become," *Ensign*, Nov. 2000, 32.

the youngest philanthropists in history. I would leave school and go live life as a wealthy independent. I had arrived.

Well, as you may have guessed, I did *not* win a million dollars. I *was*, however, introduced to the world of laser printers and TrueType fonts, which were able to mass produce very convincing letters. Publishers Clearing House had me going for a couple of hours, but my letter had the same fate of those received by my parents for so many years. Instead of becoming a young millionaire, I finished college, went to graduate school, and became a psychologist. I started a business and worked for years to get reliable referrals. Six children came in the meantime. The lessons I learned along the way have been priceless. I doubt I would have learned much of anything had I become independently wealthy at the age of 22. Working through life day by day has brought a wealth of experience that I will cherish forever. Similarly, our Father in Heaven wants us to develop His characteristics through our faith and works. He will not simply give us those celestial traits but will provide us with opportunities to learn and grow. We will become more like our forgiving Heavenly Father as we practice forgiveness in our own lives.

Our natural instinct when facing challenges is to retreat inward, and some situations devastate us so greatly that we feel we don't have the strength to forgive. Nephi gave wonderful counsel about how to respond in such situations: "Do not slacken my strength because of mine afflictions" (2 Nephi 4:29). When things go wrong and afflictions mount, he suggested, we should strive to be just as strong as before the trials came. We should improve our commitment to keep the commandments and be faithful to our covenants. Where popular wisdom would say, "Forget others; be selfish. Care for you and you alone," the gospel of Jesus Christ teaches, "Reach out; be selfless. Look for opportunities to serve those around you."

Consider the example of our Savior as He experienced the torture of crucifixion. His mother, Mary, witnessed the event. I can only imagine the personal agony she felt as she watched her first child put to death. One would think the Savior would have been primarily concerned with His own suffering in such a moment of extreme suffering. However, the scriptures record He was still looking for opportunities to comfort those He loved. The Gospel of John records the following:

> Now there stood by the cross of Jesus his mother, and his mother's sister, Mary the wife of Cleophas, and Mary Magdalene. When Jesus therefore saw his mother, and the disciple standing by, whom he loved, he saith unto his mother, Woman, behold thy son! Then saith he to the disciple, Behold thy mother! And from that hour that disciple took her unto his own home. (John 19:25–27)

Even in the midst of such great challenges, the Son of God was more concerned about others than about Himself. His commitment to be true to His mortal mission appeared to be as strong as ever, despite His afflictions. We should seek to emulate His example.

This is not to say there is no place for self-care. On the contrary, we must properly attend to our emotional needs. Yet we have missed the mark if we do this at the exclusion of caring for and being mindful of others. As we live close to the Spirit, we will know how much we can serve and provide for others without going emotionally bankrupt. We must be accountable for our own spiritual development, which includes forgiving others their trespasses against us. Elder Jörg Klebingat of the Quorum of the Seventy offered a clear, concise summary of our obligation in this regard:

> Take responsibility for your own spiritual well-being. Stop blaming others or your circumstances, stop justifying, and stop making excuses for why you may not be fully striving to be obedient. Accept that you are "free according to the flesh" and "free to choose liberty and eternal life" (2 Nephi 2:27). The Lord knows your circumstances perfectly, but He also knows perfectly well whether you simply choose not to fully live the gospel. If that is the case, be honest enough to admit it, and strive to be perfect within your own sphere of circumstances.[11]

One of the crowning traits of our Savior Jesus Christ is His capacity to freely forgive. Because He loves us and wants us to travel this life without unnecessary grief, He commands and expects us to be free with forgiveness to those around us. While it may feel like we are giving up our only power or recourse when we forgive those who have intentionally wronged us, the exact opposite will happen. Those who forgive experience a remarkable joy and peace. Relief and understanding replace anger and heartache. If we seek greater comfort and solace in life, we should seriously consider increasing our capacity to forgive others. The results in our lives will be marvelous. President Dieter F. Uchtdorf summarized this concept wonderfully: "Remember, heaven is filled with those who have this in common: They are forgiven. And they forgive."[12]

---

11 Jörg Klebingat, "Approaching the Throne of God with Confidence," *Ensign*, Nov. 2014, 35.

12 Dieter F. Uchtdorf, "The Merciful Obtain Mercy," *Ensign*, May 2012, 77.

Key Concept 4

Become the sort of person who does not harbor resentment and is quick to forgive.

QUESTIONS FOR SELF-REFLECTION

- How do I feel when I consider the commandment to forgive all people?
- What have I felt when I have been forgiven by the Savior?
- How can trying to understand others better increase my ability to forgive them?
- Do I feel justified in harboring resentment toward certain people? If so, how does this affect my overall attitude in life?

CHAPTER 7
"Wilt Thou Make Me That I May Shake at the Appearance of Sin?"

Why does sin seem so enticing at times?
Why is it so difficult to change some patterns of behavior?

Jesus went unto the mount of Olives. And early in the morning he came again into the temple, and all the people came unto him; and he sat down, and taught them. And the scribes and Pharisees brought unto him a woman taken in adultery; and when they had set her in the midst, They say unto him, Master, this woman was taken in adultery, in the very act. Now Moses in the law commanded us, that such should be stoned: but what sayest thou? This they said, tempting him, that they might have to accuse him. But Jesus stooped down, and with his finger wrote on the ground, as though he heard them not. So when they continued asking him, he lifted up himself, and said unto them, He that is without sin among you, let him first cast a stone at her. And again he stooped down, and wrote on the ground. And they which heard it, being convicted by their own conscience, went out one by one, beginning at the eldest, even unto the last: and Jesus was left alone, and the woman standing in the midst. When Jesus had lifted up himself, and saw none but the woman, he said unto her, Woman, where are those thine accusers? hath no man condemned thee? She said, No man, Lord. And Jesus said unto her, Neither do I condemn thee: go, and sin no more. (John 8:1–11)

We often associate this account with the importance of forgiveness and mercy. Yet it is equally important to recognize another principle taught by the

Master: that of forsaking sin. The command to "go, and sin no more" is essential to our journey through life. We live in a fallen world and have fallen personal natures. These conditions make us naturally susceptible to temptations and sinful desires. Nephi's lament can easily be that of us all: "I am encompassed about, because of the temptations and the sins which do so easily beset me" (2 Nephi 4:18). Understandably, he cries out to the Lord, "Wilt thou make me that I may shake at the appearance of sin?" (2 Nephi 4:31). Nephi understood the importance of learning to forsake sinful ways and the absolute necessity of involving the Savior in this process. Learning to hate sin and to seek repentance is instrumental in helping us gain the spiritual confidence to be strong in moments of personal failure.

At least one thing is certain: sin is desirable and enticing. Engaging in sinful behavior often provides very powerful and temporary pleasure and gratification. Not all sin is appealing to everyone, but every person has some sinful behavior that is difficult for them to resist. *This is very much a part of the plan of salvation.* If committing sin were not appealing in some way, then it wouldn't be a test to avoid the behavior. For example, I don't care for Brussels sprouts. I have never been tempted to eat them. You could put a full plate in front of me, waft the scent throughout the room, and I'd be perfectly fine. I could sit there all day long until the sprouts grew cold. I could resist that temptation with literally no effort. However, the results would be quite different if you were to give me a freshly grilled chicken quesadilla. The temptation to eat would grow stronger as the tantalizing smells filled the room. It would take serious resolve to resist and would be a true test of my willpower.

So it is with sin. We have to be enticed by it, or it wouldn't be an adequate test of our willingness to follow the commandments of God. Oftentimes we find certain commandments are in exact opposition to our natural desires. For those who are naturally anxious, the commandment to "doubt not, fear not" runs counter to their base instincts (D&C 6:36). Those who struggle with depression have difficulty "[hoping] for a better world" (Ether 12:4). These types of commandments, those that go against our natures, are the ones that are often the most difficult to keep. Our Heavenly Father watches our behavior very closely and is interested to observe what we will do when faced with a truly difficult choice. After all, His plan for us from the beginning is as follows: "And we will prove them herewith, to see if they will do all things whatsoever the Lord their God shall command them" (Abraham 3:25). The prophet Lehi explained how the choice between good and evil was in place from the very foundations of this earth:

And to bring about his eternal purposes in the end of man, after he had created our first parents, and the beasts of the field and the fowls of the air, and in fine, all things which are created, it must needs be that there was an opposition; even the forbidden fruit in opposition to the tree of life; the one being sweet and the other bitter. Wherefore, the Lord God gave unto man that he should act for himself. Wherefore, man could not act for himself save it should be that he was enticed by the one or the other. (2 Nephi 2:15–16)

Sometimes we think there is something wrong with us when we experience sinful desires, but having a desire for sin is part of the Father's plan. We are born into a world subject to the consequences of the Fall of Adam. We experience the effects of the natural man, which by definition is carnal, sensual, and devilish (see Mosiah 16:3). These are some of the qualities of our imperfect natures. Struggling with a natural enticement toward sin gives us a great opportunity to prove ourselves. Will we simply give in to what comes easiest? Or will we resist such urges and choose what is in harmony with the commandments of God? That is one of the great tests of life. We are born into this world with challenges and difficulties so we can be humble and choose to change through the miracle of the Atonement of Jesus Christ.

When Nephi pleads to be made to "shake at the appearance of sin," what is he asking for? I believe he wants his nature to be changed. He wants to become the type of person who sees sin with abhorrence rather than with desire. Where he would naturally desire sin and chafe at righteousness, he wants to naturally desire righteousness and find sin appalling. Is this even possible? In a world where sin is so prevalent, where immorality is championed, and where false gods abound? Can we actually change our base instincts? The answer is absolute and unequivocal: yes! Not only is it possible, but it is also a key purpose of our existence. If we go through our whole life and find we have not changed much over time, then we have missed a great opportunity.

The Book of Mormon people of King Benjamin had a transformative experience after his amazing discourse regarding the need for change and repentance.

And now, it came to pass that when king Benjamin had thus spoken to his people, he sent among them, desiring to know of his people if they believed the words which he had spoken

> unto them. And they all cried with one voice, saying: Yea, we believe all the words which thou hast spoken unto us; and also, we know of their surety and truth, because of the Spirit of the Lord Omnipotent, *which has wrought a mighty change in us, or in our hearts, that we have no more disposition to do evil, but to do good continually.* (Mosiah 5:1–2; emphasis added)

These people had a powerful spiritual event during which they felt a change in their very natures. Just like us, they were subject to the conditions of the Fall and struggled with sinful desires. Yet they were able to experience a change from their carnal, sensual natures to become more spiritual and obedient through the process of repentance. Just prior to this event, these same people had "viewed themselves in their own carnal state, even less than the dust of the earth" (Mosiah 4:2). They had begged God for forgiveness and change. While this transformation from the carnal to the spiritual is available to all of us, it comes at a significant price.

The Book of Mormon account of Aaron's mission among the Lamanites teaches us about the price of change. When Aaron taught King Lamoni's father about the plan of salvation, the great king asked what he needed to do in order to be redeemed from his fallen state. Aaron taught him the need for repentance. The king immediately petitioned God with the following words: "O God, Aaron hath told me that there is a God; and if there is a God, and if thou art God, wilt thou make thyself known unto me, *and I will give away all my sins to know thee,* and that I may be raised from the dead, and be saved at the last day" (Alma 22:18; emphasis added). It is interesting to note how just days before, the previously unrepentant king was confronted by Ammon. Ammon and the king fought, and the king's life was in jeopardy. When bargaining with Ammon to have his life spared, the king offered him up to half of his kingdom (see Alma 20:1–23). While that appeared to be a generous offer, *it was still only half.* Clearly the king's motivation in that moment had limits. Yet after being taught the gospel of Jesus Christ and feeling the humbling influence of the Spirit of the Lord, the king was willing to give away *all* of his sins to achieve forgiveness and spiritual change. The complete forsaking of sin is an essential step in being changed from one who is naturally inclined toward sin to one who becomes naturally inclined toward righteousness.

There are many scriptural references to this type of wholehearted rejection of sinful ways, including the following:

"And now, my beloved brethren, I would that ye should come unto Christ, who is the Holy One of Israel, and partake of his salvation, and the power of his redemption. Yea, come unto him, and *offer your whole souls as an offering unto him*" (Omni 1:26; emphasis added).

"For whosoever will save his life shall lose it: and *whosoever will lose his life for my sake* shall find it" (Matthew 16:25; emphasis added).

"So likewise, whosoever he be of you *that forsaketh not all that he hath*, he cannot be my disciple" (Luke 14:33; emphasis added).

"Verily I say unto you, all among them who know their hearts are honest, and are broken, and their spirits contrite, and are willing to observe their covenants by sacrifice—*yea, every sacrifice which I, the Lord, shall command*—they are accepted of me" (D&C 97:8; emphasis added).

One of Satan's prominent and widely accepted deceptions is that we cannot change who we are. He would have us believe the natural desires and inclinations we possess will be with us forever and there is nothing we can do about it. His philosophy is given some credence when we try to change our negative ways and find it is difficult. We feel his influence in those times when we try to move forward and yet find ourselves sliding backward. "See?" he chides. "I told you change was impossible. You are just that way. Better to accept it and move on than keep fighting a fight you will always lose." We have to remember that Satan is a liar and seeks our ultimate destruction. We *can* change. Not only that, we *have* to change in order to return to live with God the Father. Yet simple desire is not enough for such a transformation. This type of change is greatly facilitated through two key elements: full commitment and divine assistance.

There is a pattern in the recently referenced scriptures. Words such as *whole*, *all*, and *every* suggest the nature of the commitment we must make in order to abandon sin and seek a change of heart. We cannot hold back a portion and expect to achieve a powerful change. We must commit with our entire hearts. There is a story in the New Testament regarding Ananias and Sapphira (see Acts 5:1–10). This husband and wife lived during a time when Church members had all things in common. Personal proceeds were given to Church leaders for appropriate redistribution. Ananias and Sapphira sold a parcel of land for a certain sum. They were then expected to contribute *all* of that money to the Church. However, they secretly agreed with each other to tell Church leaders the land had sold for a lesser amount and then keep the balance of the money to themselves. Ananias went to Peter to contribute the funds. Peter asked him if the amount given was the full amount of the sale. Ananias lied and told Peter it was the full amount.

Peter detected the deception through revelation. He accused Ananias of not only lying to man but also to God, and Ananias fell dead. Peter encountered Sapphira a few hours later. She was unaware of what had just happened with her husband. Peter inquired of her regarding the sale price of the land, and she reported the same untruthful amount. Peter discovered her deception as well, and Sapphira immediately died.

That's a pretty serious consequence for holding back a portion, but the spiritual implications are clear. If we want spiritual progression, we can't hold back in the repentance process. Committing to partial change while intentionally holding on to some sins can lead to ongoing spiritual separation from God. The Savior wants us to fully abandon our sinful ways. He desires we forsake *everything* that makes us different from Him in order to show our degree of commitment.

However, do not mistake holding back a portion with failing because of weakness. The path to spiritual change will be fraught with backslides for all of us. There is a distinct difference between sliding down the mountain a few feet after losing our footing and turning around and running down the mountain. In the first case, we are doing what we can to move forward but our weakness causes missteps. In the second case, we intentionally move in a direction opposite the goal. The first case can best be described as weakness, while the second case represents rebellion. Elder Richard G. Scott provided an excellent explanation of how the Lord views these two conditions:

> The joyful news for anyone who desires to be rid of the consequences of past poor choices is that the Lord sees weaknesses differently than He does rebellion. Whereas the Lord warns that unrepented rebellion will bring punishment, when the Lord speaks of weaknesses, it is always with mercy.[13]

We are here on earth to become the type of people who seek obedience by avoiding rebellion and resisting the temptation to justify disobedience. If this disposition runs counter to our natures, then we should actively seek to change our natures through the Atonement of Jesus Christ.

Many are familiar with the Book of Mormon story of the Anti-Nephi-Lehis, who were a group of converted Lamanites. In a very dramatic example of change, they literally buried their weapons as a token that they would never again use them to fight. Thousands of them fully honored that commitment when the time of battle came. They submitted to death rather than breaking

---

13   Richard G. Scott, "Personal Strength through the Atonement of Jesus Christ," *Ensign*, Nov. 2013, 83.

their agreement. The scriptures record that these individuals were faithful for the rest of their days, never falling away from the truth (see Alma 23:6). Even more impressive than burying their weapons of war is the following: "For they became a righteous people; they did lay down the *weapons of their rebellion*, that they did not fight against God any more, neither against any of their brethren" (Alma 23:7; emphasis added). Laying down "weapons of rebellion" is comparable to forsaking sin. It is the determination to keep the commandments regardless of our natural inclinations. It is the commitment to do what is right even when this means social difficulty or rejection. It is the promise to follow God's will, even and *especially* when this conflicts with our own desires.

The Old Testament story of Lot's wife teaches a companion principle. Lot and his family were commanded to flee Sodom and Gomorrah prior to the Lord's destruction of the city. The city had become so wicked that not even ten righteous people could be found therein. Lot and his family were told to leave the city and not look back, "lest [they] be consumed" (Genesis 19:17). Contrary to the commandment, Lot's wife looked back and was turned into a pillar of salt. We do not know the reasons she looked back. Yet we know why we might. There are problems with the desire to look back, particularly when it comes to repenting and forsaking our sins.

First, we must be obedient to the commandment to forsake and leave our sins behind. Those who truly forsake do not look back at their past desires. With powerful examples, the Savior taught this principle to His disciples:

> And [Jesus] said unto another, Follow me. But he said, Lord, suffer me first to go and bury my father. Jesus said unto him, Let the dead bury their dead: but go thou and preach the kingdom of God. And another also said, Lord, I will follow thee; but let me first go bid them farewell, which are at home at my house. And Jesus said unto him, No man, having put his hand to the plough, and looking back, is fit for the kingdom of God. (Luke 9:59–62)

It is a problem to say, "Yes, I'll be obedient, but let me take care of a few things first. I'll become a committed disciple first thing tomorrow morning." When we make covenants to obey, this should not be with conditions. Our intention should be complete obedience or at least complete desire for obedience, with no looking back.

I have often made New Year's resolutions to become healthier and more fit, and I am rarely successful. Knowing that my resolution will begin on January 1, I eat like a glutton on December 31. I stuff as much chocolate desserts and cheese fondue into my mouth as I can, because the next day begins the new healthy me. I follow the feast with a nap for a king. The resolution to have a healthier lifestyle doesn't last. The only times I have been successful at having a healthier lifestyle in general have been when I have consistently eaten a healthy diet and exercised regularly. There are no gimmicks, ceremonial dates, or statements of "I'll start dieting as soon as I polish off this cheese fondue." My decision to change needs to be effective in the moment, with no fond farewells or last-minute binges. Repentance and spiritual change is similar. If we desire to become more obedient, we need to start now. There is no waiting for Sunday, next general conference, or when China is opened for missionary work. True motivation does not wait.

The second problem with the behavior of looking back is the idea that somehow our former lifetime of sin was desirable. If we miss the so-called "good times" we had before we repented, then perhaps our repentance is not complete. I remember attending a Church meeting many years ago. We were talking about the cleansing effect of baptism and receiving the gift of the Holy Ghost. One of the men in the room remarked how some people don't hear the gospel until late in life. They get baptized and confirmed and then die shortly thereafter. He thought they were somewhat fortunate, as they were able to live a lifetime of sin, have it all washed away, and have only a few years of covenant obedience left. A recent convert was in attendance. He was a man in his sixties who had been introduced to the gospel and baptized just a few years earlier. As he was a prime example of one who got to live the so-called good life and then get baptized later, I asked him, "What do you think of your life before finding the gospel?" He promptly responded, "I would have given anything to have found the gospel fifty years earlier; it has been the best thing in my life."

If we think sinning will somehow bring happiness, forsaking sin will be very difficult. We will find it challenging to change our ways if we perceive the commandments as restrictive. Alma's counsel is as applicable today as it was decades before the birth of Christ: "Behold, I say unto you, wickedness never was happiness" (Alma 41:10). Although sin can bring temporary pleasure and satisfaction, it will never bring happiness. It will never create the feelings of joy and satisfaction that the righteous experience. Some would disagree, saying, "I've seen my friends who don't belong to the Church and who do not keep the commandments; they seem pretty happy to me." Whatever pleasant experience disobedience yields is not true happiness. It is completely temporary. In order to test our faith to see if we will repent, the Lord does not always let us feel the full consequences of sin right away. In addition, Satan is able to sustain the disobedient for a time. Yet his support will cease eventually and with certainty. With the Book of Mormon anti-Christ Korihor as a chilling example, Mormon gave this warning: "And thus we see that the devil will not support his children at the last day, but doth speedily drag them down to hell" (Alma 30:60). If we think there is happiness in committing sin, we must reconsider. Sinful ways will never yield the happiness the Lord wants us to experience. We aren't likely to completely forsake those things we believe are somewhat desirable. As such, we must change any attitudes we possess that would support disobedience. We have to forsake our sins in order to move forward and find true happiness.

Jesus Christ is the perfect example in forsaking sin. We know He was tempted, but He did not succumb (see Matthew 4:1–11). It is important to note that it is not sinful to be tempted. Just because we have a temporary desire to do something unrighteous does not mean we have sinned. However, it *is* sinful to break the commandments by yielding to temptation. The Apostle Paul commented regarding the unyielding obedience of our Savior: "Seeing then that we have a great high priest, that is passed into the heavens, Jesus the Son of God, let us hold fast our profession. For we have not an high priest which cannot be touched with the feeling of our infirmities; *but was in all points tempted like as we are, yet without sin*" (Hebrews 4:14–15; emphasis added).

Some will remark, "I've tried to abandon my sins. I've been on my knees in tears, pleading for forgiveness. I've promised Heavenly Father I'd never do it again. I've felt His love and the sweet joy of being cleansed from sin. But then I've done it again. I've committed the same sin I promised I would never do." Although it seems somewhat contradictory, I hope you have had a similar experience to this. If you haven't, you are missing out on one of the greatest lessons you can learn in this life. I don't believe we are meant to succeed at the first try. I think periodic failure is part of the plan. Not only will the ultimate result still be the same as if we defeated all our weaknesses with one attempt, but we will also develop incredible godlike characteristics. The words of C. S. Lewis, when he spoke of chastity, can apply to anything with which we struggle:

> We may, indeed, be sure that perfect chastity—like perfect charity—will not be obtained by any merely human efforts. You must ask for God's help. Even when you have done so, it may seem to you for a long time that no help, or less help than you need, is being given. Never mind. After each failure, ask forgiveness, pick yourself up, and try again. Very often what God first helps us towards is not the virtue itself but just this

power of always trying again. For however important chastity (or courage, or truthfulness, or any other virtue) may be, this process trains us in habits of the soul which are more important still. It cures our illusions about ourselves and teaches us to depend upon God. We learn, on the one hand, that we cannot trust ourselves even in our best moments, and, on the other, that we need not despair even in our worst, for our failures are forgiven. The only fatal thing is to sit down content with anything less than perfection.[14]

I believe there are times when God deliberately overloads us. He wants us to lift as hard as we can and still find our strength exhausted. It is in those moments, when we are tired, weak, and humble, that we can turn to Him and utilize His strength in addition to our own. Some will say, "But the scriptures teach I'll never have a problem I can't handle; God will never command anything that I can't overcome." That is absolutely true. Yet I am unaware of any statements in those scriptures that say, "You'll be able to do it with *your* strength alone." As we try to forsake our sins and struggle with ongoing weakness, we become prepared for greater spiritual growth. In our desperation, we reach out to Him, take His hand, and *then* the miracles begin. As C. S. Lewis noted in the previous quote, we need to be cured of our illusions about ourselves and understand our complete need for heavenly dependence.

The price to become a changed person who shakes at the appearance of sin is twofold. We must forsake our sins by abandoning the attitude that wickedness is sometimes happiness. This leads to repentance with full purpose of heart. Then we must partner with the Savior, keeping our covenants with sincere diligence. We choose to rely on Him to sustain us in our weaknesses and shortcomings. When He commanded the adulterous woman to "go, and sin no more," He asked her to walk a difficult and demanding path. He invites all to walk that same path. Please realize He is not asking us to walk that path alone. If we will permit Him, He will walk that path with us every step of the way. *After all, He has already walked it on our behalf.* He is thrilled to show us the journey to safety. How I love our merciful, compassionate Redeemer, who is truly "the way, the truth, and the life" (John 14:6).

Key Concept 5
Learn to forsake sin and choose righteousness through developing a partnership with the Savior.

---

14   C. S. Lewis, *Mere Christianity* (New York: HarperOne, 1952), 101–102.

QUESTIONS FOR SELF-REFLECTION

- How do I feel when I consider that human weakness is actually a part of Heavenly Father's plan?
- When change is difficult, do I find myself making excuses for negative behavior? What can I do to change that?
- What are my feelings regarding the power of the Atonement of Jesus Christ?
- Do I believe the Atonement of Jesus Christ can completely and permanently change negative characteristics?

CHAPTER 8
"My Heart Is Broken and My Spirit Is Contrite"

Why do we have weakness?
What are we willing to sacrifice to have a stronger relationship with God?

FORSAKING SIN IS A NECESSARY step in spiritual progression. However, it is an insufficient step in and of itself. Unless we are able to fill our hearts with heavenly characteristics, removing evil desires will not be effective or long-lasting. Nephi gave some insight into this process as he made this impassioned request of the Lord: "May the gates of hell be shut continually before me, because that my heart is broken and my spirit is contrite! O Lord, wilt thou not shut the gates of thy righteousness before me, that I may walk in the path of the low valley, that I may be strict in the plain road!" (2 Nephi 4:32). He understood that the path to spiritual confidence and resilience includes not only avoiding sin but also seeking righteousness. We can follow his example as we seek for greater personal strength.

In his request, Nephi asked for two things. He requested the gates of hell be shut before him. He also wanted the gates of righteousness to open for him. Yet after each request he indicated what *he* will do in order to qualify for these blessings. He pledged that his heart would be broken and his spirit contrite. He committed to walk in the path of the low valley and to be strict in the plain road. Walking in the path of the low valley suggests being humble, while being strict in the plain road refers to being obedient. After removing evil desires from our nature, we would do well to replace them with humility and obedience. Our base natures are not inherently humble or obedient, so what must we do in order to acquire the godlike characteristic of humble obedience?

The key is in the phrase, *broken heart and contrite spirit*. While this concept is minimally present in Old Testament scriptures, it was not until after the death and resurrection of the Savior that He made this idea very explicit: "And ye shall offer up unto me no more the shedding of blood; yea, your sacrifices and your burnt offerings shall be done away, for I will accept none of your sacrifices and your burnt offerings. And ye shall offer for a sacrifice unto me a broken heart and a contrite spirit" (3 Nephi 9:19–20).

The children of Israel were required to make numerous sacrifices as they worshipped under the law of Moses. This helped them look forward to the great atoning sacrifice of the Lord Jesus Christ. The rituals associated with these sacrifices were complex. The sacrifices themselves helped the Israelites remember their God. Faithful execution of the sacrifices also provided remission of sins. When a person performed such a sacrifice, they often had to use an animal they provided themselves. This made it more personal and represented their willingness to give up something of their own in exchange for something from God.

Contemporary followers of Jesus Christ are no longer required to make blood sacrifices. They are asked to make an offering of a broken heart and contrite spirit. What does it mean to have a broken heart and contrite spirit? Elder Bruce D. Porter of the Quorum of the Seventy gave this explanation:

> The Savior's perfect submission to the Eternal Father is the very essence of a broken heart and a contrite spirit. Christ's example teaches us that a broken heart is an eternal attribute of godliness. When our hearts are broken, we are completely open to the Spirit of God and recognize our dependence on Him for all that we have and all that we are. The sacrifice so entailed is a sacrifice of pride in all its forms. Like malleable clay in the hands of a skilled potter, the brokenhearted can be molded and shaped in the hands of the Master.[15]

We now offer our hearts and wills to God instead of offering animals. We humbly accept His commands and follow them with full purpose of heart. This requires humility as we acknowledge the need to change. We are very unlikely to change our behavior if we do not believe we need to change. As a psychologist, I have worked with troubled youth many times. In most cases, the youth has made choices contrary to the parents' desires. The parents bring the youth in for counseling and essentially tell me it is my job to "fix" their child. I've sat down with many youth and asked why they have come to counseling. In almost every case, the response is, "Because my parents made me." I'll ask what changes they think need to happen in their life. They'll say, "I don't need to change anything. My parents need to develop a better attitude." Such sessions tend to move very

15   Bruce D. Porter, "A Broken Heart and a Contrite Spirit," *Ensign*, Nov. 2007, 32.

slowly, because the client does not believe he has a problem. As a result, he has no desire to change. Trying to convince him of any need for change is usually a fruitless process. The only hope for progress is if the youth decides he *wants* to change; then we can move forward.

Being humble is essential in the process of personal change. Sometimes we realize on our own that we need to change our lives and make better choices. Other times those around us see the need for change and encourage us to modify our path. Those who are humble are able to incorporate such feedback and look for opportunities to grow. Those who lack humility often get angry at such suggestions and therefore resist change. Those who choose humility tend to become more and more humble, leading to greater changes and the development of more Christlike characteristics. Those who choose pride tend to become more and more prideful, leading to a slow disintegration of the spiritual talents they once possessed. Humility is the antidote to pride. We will find pride occupies less space in our hearts as we fill our lives with service toward others and consideration of their needs.

We must change our lives to achieve a broken heart and contrite spirit. The war in heaven was fought in part over the preservation of agency: that precious gift that permits us to reason and to choose between good and evil. Change can be very difficult. However, pride is not the only reason we are hesitant to change. We also resist change because we are creatures of habit. When we do the same thing repeatedly, our brains adapt to those patterns. Researchers have discovered that when people form habits of behavior, brain activity decreases for those specific behaviors. That is to say, once you become experienced in doing something, your brain does not need to fully engage at every step of the process. The brain is usually active at the beginning and end of those tasks, but during the middle there is a sense of autopilot that seems to take over. I have a personal experience that highlights this fact.

Many years ago, I worked for a counseling agency. I worked until late in the evening several nights a week. I didn't need to consult a map or ask for directions to get home in the evening. I knew the way. I knew it so fully that I think my brain was half off during the drive. Before I knew it, I would pull into our driveway. One evening around five o'clock, my wife called and asked if I would pick up milk on my way home. I told her I would be happy to do it. At nine P.M. when I left work, I got in the car and went straight to our house. When I walked in, my wife asked, "Did you get the milk?" Of course I hadn't. I had completely forgotten. I drove back to the store, the very store I passed on the way home from work, and purchased the milk. When I'd told my wife earlier that I would get milk, I had every intention to do so. Yet when I got into the car, habit took over and my brain went into autopilot mode. I drove straight home like I usually did.

A few weeks later, my wife called again and made the same request. She wanted me to purchase milk on the way home. Remembering my prior failure to follow through, I put a reminder note on my desk. As I was completing the necessary paperwork for the day, I inadvertently covered the reminder note with other papers. Nine o'clock came, and I got into my car and drove straight home, passing the grocery store without a thought. When I arrived at the house and pulled into the driveway, I suddenly remembered I had forgotten to get the milk. I backed out of the driveway and went back to the store. A few weeks later, my wife called *again* at five P.M. and made the familiar request for milk. I was happy to oblige as usual. But this time, I wrote a note on a piece of paper, went out to my car, and taped the note to the middle of the steering wheel. I am pleased to report I did *not* forget the milk on that occasion.

Habits of behavior are difficult to change, especially those that have been in place for many years. Our brains *will* adapt to new patterns, but only after such patterns have been clearly established. You will *not* be able to break a twenty-year habit in one day, even with the best of intentions. Your brain will resist the change. Yet change *will* come over time and with consistent commitment to new patterns. This process will not only help you break bad habits, but it can also help create good ones. You can train your brain so that good behaviors become just as difficult to quit as the bad behaviors used to be. However, consistent and disciplined behavior is required to achieve such change. Do not abandon your efforts to change old behaviors if you encounter failure or resistance. Instead, expect plenty of setbacks and missteps as part of this process. Keep trying and you will find old habits yield to new ones in time.

Unfortunately, we don't just have brain chemistry to contend with when trying to manage our lives. We also have our personalities and histories that affect our perceptions of our abilities to change. Sometimes we think we cannot change, especially if past efforts have met with failure. Sometimes we are afraid to change because we become miserably comfortable in our current situation. In addition, Satan actively campaigns against us, telling us we cannot improve. He also works to accentuate our fears of change. He suggests that although our current situation may not be ideal, it is certainly better than stepping into the darkness for an unknown period of time.

In his allegorical book *The Great Divorce*, C. S. Lewis tells the story of a man who is confronted with the choice to change his life. The character is faced with the option to change for the better or continue his somewhat miserable existence. While the man debates his options, an angel approaches. The angel invites him to "come to the mountains," which represents going to the presence of God. While the man thinks that would be a good plan, he claims he cannot go on the journey. You see, he has a red lizard on his shoulder. The lizard has been with him for a long time. To complicate matters, the likes of that lizard would never be welcome in God's presence.

The angel offers to kill the lizard, thus freeing the man from the burden and allowing him to start his journey to heaven. The man protests somewhat. The lizard protests even more. Frantically, the lizard tells the man that the angel can indeed kill him. The lizard warns that the man would be devastated to lose him, as they have been together for so long. The angel moves closer and again asks the man if he can kill the lizard. The man continues to debate and eventually exclaims how killing the lizard would likely kill him as well, as they are so interconnected. The angel asks, "What if the process did kill you?" The man responds that it would be better to die than to continue to live with the burden. He permits the angel to destroy the lizard.

The process that follows is quite painful for the man. At one point, he thinks he is going to die. However, he does not die but becomes stronger and more independent. The lizard transforms as well. It changes from a whining, tempting nuisance to a glorious stallion. The transformed man then mounts the stallion, and they ride off toward the presence of God together.[16] This wonderful story has always reminded me of the following scripture: "And if men come unto me I will show unto them their weakness. I give unto men weakness that they may be humble; and my grace is sufficient for all men that humble themselves before me; for if they humble themselves before me, and have faith in me, then will I make weak things become strong unto them" (Ether 12:27).

This is a familiar verse to many Latter-day Saints, often referred to as the "weaknesses become strengths" scripture. That transformation is contingent upon humility and faith in Jesus Christ. What many fail to realize is the doctrine contained in the second sentence of the verse: "I give unto men weakness that they may be humble." The desires of the natural man and woman are typically contrary to the will of God. We know such feelings and thoughts are part of the consequences that resulted from the Fall of Adam. Yet this scripture teaches that at least some of our weaknesses and flaws stem from human frailty that comes from God. This weakness is a gift from a loving Heavenly Father. Some would protest and say, "How could a loving God intentionally give me something that

---

16   C. S. Lewis, *The Great Divorce* (New York: HarperOne, 1946), 106–112.

would result in personal struggles? Why would He give me challenges that could possibly lead me away from Him?" In His eternal wisdom, Heavenly Father knows the tremendous growth that comes from the righteous endurance of suffering. Why do soccer coaches make their teams do so much running as part of their training? Because they are well aware that conditioning is crucial for the upcoming competitions. You might have great soccer skills, but if you can't run up and down a huge field for about ninety minutes, you aren't going to be effective. God permits us to experience challenges that will help us perform well when difficulties come. He does this to prepare us for life with Him in His kingdom.

Sister Neill F. Marriott described a personal example that gives valuable insight into why the Lord gives us weakness:

> Some years ago our family encountered a major challenge. I went to the temple and there prayed earnestly for help. I was given a moment of truth. I received a clear impression of my weaknesses, and I was shocked. In that spiritually instructive moment, I saw a prideful woman doing things her own way, not necessarily the Lord's way, and privately taking credit for any so-called accomplishment. I knew I was looking at myself. I cried out in my heart to Heavenly Father and said, "I don't want to be that woman, but how do I change?" Through the pure spirit of revelation in the temple, I was taught of my utter need for a Redeemer. I turned immediately to the Savior Jesus Christ in my thoughts and felt my anguish melt away and a great hope spring up in my heart. He was my only hope, and I longed to cling only to Him. It was clear to me that a self-absorbed natural woman "is an enemy to God" (Mosiah 3:19) and to people in her sphere of influence. In the temple that day I learned it was only through the Atonement of Jesus Christ that my prideful nature could change and that I would be enabled to do good. I felt His love keenly, and I knew He would teach me by the Spirit and change me if I gave my heart to Him, holding back nothing.[17]

The Savior will help us change and reach our true heavenly potential as we recognize our weaknesses and humbly turn to Him. Humility does not come naturally to most people. For some it is a very difficult attitude to adopt. Yet as human beings we should be familiar with the concept that we cannot survive

17   Neill F. Marriott, "Sharing Your Light," *Ensign*, Nov. 2014, 118.

without some sort of help. Many animal species are independently capable within weeks of their birth, while human beings are quite the opposite. Human infants would perish if not immediately cared for, fed, and nurtured after birth. They cannot move from place to place. They cannot feed themselves. They cannot defend against predators. Humans become self-sufficient only after many years of dependence. We then go through several decades during which we are able to care for ourselves. In old age, we are again dependent upon others for our survival. I believe this is by design. It is a constant reminder that we can't survive on our own. We need to reach out for something more. Those who reach out to the Savior in humility and faith can find strength they never knew. In so many cases, it is that divinely appointed weakness that leads us back to God.

As you consider your various weaknesses, remember that many of them have been given to you through God's wisdom. Life's challenges often come from two sources: poor choices or divine appointment. Do your best to avoid the challenges that come from poor choices. While we can still learn from such experiences, the learning often comes at the cost of unnecessary pain and suffering. It's like saying, "I know they have excellent medical procedures to reattach severed limbs. I think I'll chop my arm off and then go get surgery to put it back on." While medical science can correct such accidents, who would intentionally harm themselves with that in mind? Everything about the process would be very painful and could be avoided with better decision-making. Don't wander into forbidden spiritual pathways thinking, "Oh, I can always repent." It is the spiritual equivalent of chopping your arm off and going to the surgeon. While you can be made whole again, the process will be painful and could have been avoided altogether through obedience to God's laws and commandments.

All will struggle with weakness and challenges. As this happens, Satan will try to persuade you to follow fruitless paths. He does this because he is acutely aware of the purpose behind your struggles. He knows how difficulties have the potential to yield great happiness and peace if you follow the Lord's direction. He will try to get you to question why and even to develop hostile feelings toward God. Elder Richard G. Scott gave counsel regarding how to respond to the trials we will encounter:

> When you face adversity, you can be led to ask many questions. Some serve a useful purpose; others do not. To ask, Why does this have to happen to me? Why do I have to suffer this, now? What have I done to cause this? will lead you into blind alleys. It really does no good to ask questions that reflect opposition

to the will of God. Rather ask, What am I to do? What am I to learn from this experience? What am I to change? Whom am I to help? How can I remember my many blessings in times of trial? Willing sacrifice of deeply held personal desires in favor of the will of God is very hard to do. Yet, when you pray with real conviction, "Please let me know Thy will" and "May Thy will be done," you are in the strongest position to receive the maximum help from your loving Father.[18]

It is entirely possible for us to have the gates of hell shut before us, with the gates of righteousness open for our benefit (see 2 Nephi 4:32). However, the price for these blessings is our humility and obedience. We will find our hearts filled with a love of God and His commandments as we rid ourselves of disobedience and pride. We will rejoice in following His law. Sin will become less and less enticing over time. Truly, our natures will begin the process of shedding the natural man. We will start to become the sort of people who will feel very comfortable in the presence of our Father in Heaven and His Son Jesus Christ.

Key Concept 6
Recognize and accept personal weaknesses and humbly submit to God's will.

QUESTIONS FOR SELF-REFLECTION
- What is my typical reaction when others provide constructive criticism of my behavior?
- Do I tend to view personal challenges as liabilities or opportunities for change?
- What will it take for me to invest the mental and emotional energy to change longstanding patterns of negative behavior?
- How can the Atonement of Jesus Christ help me gain greater capacity to face the difficulties of life?

---

18   Richard G. Scott, "Trust in the Lord," *Ensign*, Nov. 1995, 17.

CHAPTER 9
"Yea, My God Will Give Me, If I Ask Not Amiss"

What does God want us to pray for?
How can we know Heavenly Father's will for us?

NEPHI CONCLUDES HIS INSPIRING PSALM with the following statement: "Yea, I know that God will give liberally to him that asketh. Yea, my God will give me, if I ask not amiss; therefore I will lift up my voice unto thee; yea, I will cry unto thee, my God, the rock of my righteousness. Behold, my voice shall forever ascend up unto thee, my rock and mine everlasting God" (2 Nephi 4:35). We can progress spiritually and endure our trials well as we learn to understand the will of God and then seek for those things that will help us grow.

The concept "ask and ye shall receive" is familiar to followers of Jesus Christ. He has always commanded His people to reach out to Him in faith and trust, asking for those things they need. In the Sermon on the Mount, Jesus explained why blessings will come to those who ask of God: "Or what man is there of you, whom if his son ask bread, will he give him a stone? Or if he ask a fish, will he give him a serpent? If ye then, being evil, know how to give good gifts unto your children, how much more shall your Father which is in heaven give good things to them that ask him?" (Matthew 7:9–11).

In this scripture, Jesus seems to draw attention to the difference between our fallen natures and God's exalted nature. In addition, He emphasizes how our Father in Heaven is merciful and kind to those who ask things of Him. Jesus is saying, "If you, as a mortal and imperfect being, would give appropriately and generously to your own child, how much more will Heavenly Father, being exalted and perfect, give good things to you if you will ask Him?"

Nephi seems to understand this concept. He knows God will give liberally to those who ask. However, his next statement is worthy of additional exploration. What does it mean when he says he knows God will give to him if he "asks not amiss"? In other words, Nephi seems to say, "I know God will give me what I ask for, as long as I don't ask for something I shouldn't." Does the invitation to "ask and receive" come with qualifiers?

It stands to reason that some things should *not* be requested in prayer. Most of these are common sense. For example, we shouldn't ask God for something that would benefit us at the detriment of others. I used to run cross-country in high school. I was never very good, mostly because I didn't train as hard as my fellow runners. Suppose I had trained for a race with mediocre preparation. I could still pray for Heavenly Father to help me perform to the best of my abilities. However, to ask God to cause everyone in front of me to get sick, fall down, or quit the race early so that I could win would not be appropriate, nor would it be granted. That is not the way Heavenly Father typically works with us.

Additionally, we should not pray for blessings that would circumvent God's plan for His children. For example, we know we are on earth to work, learn, and grow through trial and tribulation. Let's say I were to pray for a blessing of ten million dollars to magically appear in my bank account. That would be an ill-advised request. One *could* pray for wealth and might be blessed with a desire to work, a motivation to save, and a decreased appetite for the vain things of the world. The Lord will rarely give us things that would keep us from learning essential lessons in this life. While that could bring some short-term gratification, it would slow our spiritual growth.

These examples are obvious things we shouldn't pray for. However, there are situations that are more difficult to determine. What if you are looking for a new job? Is it the will of the Lord for you to keep your current job or get a new one? What about considering a move to a new location? Does the Lord want you to stay where you are or make the move? Many times in my life, I have prayed for a good thing to happen and the opposite occurred. While I was initially disappointed, *in time* I realized how the eventual outcome was a blessing. In most cases, I received a greater blessing than what I initially prayed for.

For some people, this can be a bit of a quandary. We might ask, "How do I know what to pray for? I don't want to ask for something Heavenly Father doesn't want me to have, but how do I know what that is?" This can become even more difficult when personal emotions become involved. Learning to recognize the voice of the Holy Ghost in one's life is a very subtle and extended process. It can be easy to misinterpret emotional excitement as spiritual confirmation.

I mentioned in the preface that our oldest son came home from the Provo Missionary Training Center on a clinical medical release. He had served only eight weeks of his two-year mission to that point. My wife and I were greatly surprised to discover he would return home for an undetermined period of time. We found out about this situation on a Friday evening. We flew to Utah right away to pick him up. As my wife and I were on the plane, my thoughts were consumed with what was going to happen. I was sure the missionary staff had overreacted. After all, they didn't know my son. If I was able to reason with them, they would surely understand their mistake and allow our son to stay. In reading my journal entry from that day, it is clear I was conflicted and worried. I remember being on the plane and praying the Lord would fix things so our son could remain at the MTC and serve his mission as originally planned. I also remember praying in the car in the MTC parking lot on Saturday morning before we went in to visit with the district president. I prayed they would allow him to stay. It seemed like the right thing. I mean, shouldn't missionaries be blessed to serve the full period of their missions without interruption? We had tried to be obedient and good parents; why would this happen to us? Surely the Lord would grant the righteous desire of my heart—to have my son remain in the mission field and complete his period of service.

The Lord did *not* answer my specific request in that moment. Several hours later, we were headed back to Washington with our son. Now, years after the fact, I look back and see all the growth that came from the experience. I am confident the Lord's will *was* done. God's plan was to have our son come home, for all of us to struggle for a while, and for great blessings to result. I thought I was praying for a good thing when I asked Heavenly Father to allow my son to stay in the MTC. However, that was not the will of the Lord at the time. Greater blessings were in store. Eventually, our son returned to the mission field stronger and more resilient. Our whole family grew from the trials we endured. The blessings we received were tremendous. As usual, the path to such blessings required pain and tribulation. Nephi stated, "God will give me, if I ask not amiss" (2 Nephi 4:35). God was not going to grant my original request to keep my son on a mission, because it wasn't the best thing at the time.

Fortunately, our Father in Heaven is very merciful and does not always give us what we pray for. He lovingly and thoughtfully blesses us with appropriate experiences based on what will encourage our greatest development. This can result in frustration on our part. We may wonder why our prayers aren't being answered, at least in the way *we* want them to be answered. This can be particularly vexing when we really think we are praying for the right thing. Oftentimes our emotions can cloud our judgment and even masquerade as feelings of the Spirit. On that Saturday morning, I *felt good* about our son staying in the MTC. Clearly, those were my own feelings and not the will of the Lord.

The concept of aligning our will to the will of the Father is a necessary step in spiritual progression. To *align* means to modify something so that it fits or agrees with something else. In order to align our will with the will of Heavenly Father, we have to know His will in the first place. The life of a Book of Mormon prophet named Nephi—not the son of Lehi but one who lived hundreds of years after him—provides a good example of aligning one's will with God.

This Nephi was a prophet who lived a few decades prior to the birth of Jesus Christ. He was a very faithful man who had the challenge of ministering to an extremely wicked people. There is an amazing account in which he is praying in his garden. A large multitude hears his prayer and gathers together. Among other things, they confront Nephi and accuse him of conspiracy regarding a recent political murder. Through the power of God, Nephi miraculously reveals the true culprits and confounds the multitude. The group disperses, and Nephi is left to himself (see Helaman 7–9). As he ponders on the events that just happened, he receives the following revelation:

> Blessed art thou, Nephi, for those things which thou hast done; for I have beheld how thou hast with unwearyingness declared the word, which I have given unto thee, unto this people. And thou hast not feared them, and hast not sought thine own life, but hast sought my will, and to keep my commandments. And now, because thou hast done this with such unwearyingness, behold, I will bless thee forever; and I will make thee mighty in word and in deed, in faith and in works; yea, even that all things shall be done unto thee according to thy word, *for thou shalt not ask that which is contrary to my will.* (Helaman 10:4–5; emphasis added)

Nephi is given considerable power, to the point where everything he asks will be done. I used to think the statement, "for thou shalt not ask that which is contrary to my will" was a command. In other words, I thought the Lord was saying, "Nephi, I'm giving you this power, but you'd better not ask for anything that is against my will." I have since come to believe the Lord was simply reiterating Nephi's existing commitment. What I think the Lord was saying is, "Nephi, I'm giving you this power because I know you very well. I know that you won't ask for anything against my will. I can trust you." Nephi had aligned his will with God's will, and therefore, God could trust him, with great confidence.

What is the process of aligning our wills to the will of Heavenly Father? How do we change from being a person who resists obedience to a person who routinely follows heavenly direction? The answer lies in an ordinance well-known to faithful Latter-day Saints—the sacrament.

> O God, the Eternal Father, we ask thee in the name of thy Son, Jesus Christ, to bless and sanctify this bread to the souls of all those who partake of it, that they may eat in remembrance of the body of thy Son, and witness unto thee, O God, the Eternal Father, that they are willing to take upon them the name of thy Son, and always remember him and keep his commandments which he has given them; that they may always have his Spirit to be with them. Amen. (D&C 20:77)

The ordinance of the sacrament typically happens on a weekly basis. Many members of The Church of Jesus Christ of Latter-day Saints have participated in this ordinance hundreds or thousands of times over the course of their lives. When we participate in this ordinance, we make three separate commitments and then receive a promised blessing. We commit to be willing to take upon us the name of Jesus Christ, always remember Jesus Christ, and keep the commandments Jesus Christ has given to us. We are promised to always have the Spirit of God with us as we faithfully fulfill these terms. Consider how each of these commitments can help us align our wills with the will of Heavenly Father.

What does it mean to be willing to take upon us the name of Jesus Christ? This is more than merely acknowledging a membership in His Church or even testifying that He is the Son of God. Elder Dallin H. Oaks explained as follows: "When we witness our *willingness* to take upon us the name of Jesus Christ, we are signifying our commitment to do all that we can to achieve eternal life in the kingdom of our Father. We are expressing our candidacy—our determination to strive for—exaltation in the celestial kingdom."[19]

Being willing to take upon us the name of Christ is a manifestation of our desire to leave behind the things of this world and seek for the things of heaven. We no longer covet temporary pleasures and satisfaction but are willing to make needed sacrifices in order to receive the blessings God has promised to the faithful.

When preparing to give what was likely his final formal address to his people, Book of Mormon prophet King Benjamin told them he would give

---

19   Dallin H. Oaks, "Taking upon Us the Name of Jesus Christ," *Ensign*, May 1985, 82.

them a name by which they could be distinguished from others. As the people listened to his words, they were motivated to repent. They covenanted with God to be obedient to His commandments. In consequence of their righteous desires, King Benjamin told them they would be called the children of Christ (see Mosiah 5:7). He went on to explain what that meant:

> And under this head ye are made free, and there is no other head whereby ye can be made free. There is no other name given whereby salvation cometh; therefore, I would that ye should take upon you the name of Christ, all you that have entered into the covenant with God that ye should be obedient unto the end of your lives. And it shall come to pass that whosoever doeth this shall be found at the right hand of God, for he shall know the name by which he is called; for he shall be called by the name of Christ. And now it shall come to pass, that whosoever shall not take upon him the name of Christ must be called by some other name; therefore, he findeth himself on the left hand of God. And I would that ye should remember also, that this is the name that I said I should give unto you that never should be blotted out, except it be through transgression; therefore, take heed that ye do not transgress, that the name be not blotted out of your hearts. I say unto you, I would that ye should remember to retain the name written always in your hearts, that ye are not found on the left hand of God, but that ye hear and know the voice by which ye shall be called, and also, the name by which he shall call you. *For how knoweth a man the master whom he has not served, and who is a stranger unto him, and is far from the thoughts and intents of his heart?* (Mosiah 5:8–13; emphasis added)

King Benjamin's remarks create a good bridge between the first sacramental commitment to be willing to take upon us the name of Jesus Christ and the third commitment, to keep His commandments. In order to align our wills with the will of God, we need to know the will of God in the first place. How do we come to know His will? We can begin to understand His will by developing a relationship with Him. Most of us know the likes, dislikes, and other preferences of a good friend. As relationships grow and mature, we learn a lot about the other person. Learning the will of God is no different. The more we come to know our Father in Heaven, the more we will understand His will for us. King Benjamin rightly reasons that those who do not serve the Master will probably be unaware of the "thoughts and intents of his heart." In other words, if we don't have a relationship with the Savior, we will be unlikely to understand His will.

Another of the sacramental commitments is to keep His commandments. It seems straightforward: surely those who obey the commandments also bend their wills to the will of the Father. Yet there are situations in which this is not always the case. Acts of obedience are not always driven by humble submission. I had the great blessing of teaching early morning seminary for several years, one of the most wonderful experiences of my life. It is remarkable that adolescents will get up extra early to attend an hour of religious instruction before school. Sleep is precious to them. To see them make such a sacrifice inspired me. One might look at a group of regular seminary attendees and say, "That is a really faithful group of youth who have aligned their wills with God's." For some students, this is an accurate statement.

Yet it was clear to me that some students were there for reasons other than submitting their will to divine direction. Some were there for the social aspect. Some were there for the promise of possible admission to a Latter-day Saint university. Some were there because their parents expected it. Others were there because their parents threatened them with punishment for nonattendance. One could safely conclude that even though these young men and women faithfully attended seminary, their motivations were numerous, perhaps some more noble than others. Like these seminary students, we obey the commandments for various reasons. Sometimes we obey out of pure love for God. Other times we obey in order to gain favor with man, to promote an agenda, or to satisfy our own needs. The ancient prophet Mormon gave good insight into this phenomenon: "For behold, if a man being evil giveth a gift, he doeth it grudgingly; wherefore it is counted unto him the same as if he had retained the gift; wherefore he is counted evil before God. And likewise also is it counted evil unto a man, if he shall pray and not with real intent of heart; yea, and it profiteth him nothing, for God receiveth none such" (Moroni 7:8–9).

Mormon explained how righteous behavior done with insincere intent is of little value. We should strive to keep the commandments for the right reasons. Aligning our wills with God's helps us grow closer to Him. This is particularly true as we keep His commandments out of submission and love. It will also help us understand Him and His desires for us. This will assist us in our prayers. The more in tune we are with the Holy Ghost, the more we will know what to pray for and what path the Lord would have us take.

When I first started teaching seminary, I saw this as a daunting challenge. I had seen enough people sleeping through nine o'clock sacrament meeting to know that trying to teach the gospel *three hours earlier* would be difficult at best. Teaching adolescents presented even greater difficulties. How could I sustain their attention? I came up with what I believed were some pretty cool and novel ideas. As I prepared these lessons, I thought, "Man, these students are going to really like this! They'll tell their friends how Brother Morgan is a great seminary teacher."

I taught a few of those lessons. *They bombed.* I'd seen better attention and interest in geometry classes. The material was stiff, and the Spirit was minimally present. As I reflected on what went wrong, I realized two things relating to my motivation. First, I wanted to entertain the students. Entertainment can sometimes be a byproduct of gospel instruction, but it should not be the focus. Second, I wanted them to like me. Focusing on *my* emotional needs blinded me to the true needs of the youth. I did not have a great seminary experience until I corrected my motivation. Although I'd been obedient by fulfilling my calling, my capacity to be blessed was limited by my misguided intentions. While doing what is right is important, we should also strive to have the right motivation for doing so.

The remaining sacramental promise is to always remember the Savior. This has powerful potential to help us align our will with God's by helping us focus on what is truly important. Life is full of distractions. Some of these are productive and necessary parts of our daily existence. Others are evil and serve to move us off the path. It is easy to lose sight of our celestial goals as we go about our daily responsibilities. I would think any faithful Latter-day Saint would say their top priority is to make it back to the presence of Father in Heaven. Yet moment to moment, problems complicate our ability to focus on that goal. "[Loving] one another" (John 13:34) is hampered by the person who cut us off in traffic. "[Standing] as witnesses of God" (Mosiah 18:9) is challenged by desires to gain social acceptance. "[Being] not afraid, only [believing]" (Mark 5:36) is derailed by fears and uncertainties in life. It is easier to stay in harmony with the Savior's will if we constantly have Him as our focus and continually remember His love and suffering for us. Regular reflection on the life of the Savior will fill our minds with thoughts of His teachings. This will help us choose righteously and with good intent.

The blessing to those who faithfully abide by the three sacramental promises is to "always have His Spirit to be with them." This could be one of most underappreciated promises extended to Latter-day Saints. In the Book of Mormon, Jesus Christ appeared to the inhabitants of ancient America. He descended from heaven to their temple in a city called Bountiful. Had we been alive during that time and seen the Savior and felt the marks in His hands and feet, we would have been thrilled! Like the others there, we likely would have wept as He announced His departure. I'm certain we would have hoped He would stay a little longer so we could continue to enjoy His ministry. What an incredible blessing it would have been to be in the presence of God!

Yet those who keep their baptismal covenants are promised to have the continual presence of the Holy Ghost, who is part of the Godhead. His influence penetrates the veil and causes our spirits to resonate with divine remembrance. His witness of truth is so significant that the only unforgivable sin in this life or the next is to blaspheme against Him. While most members of The Church of Jesus Christ of Latter-day Saints may never have the privilege of being in the physical presence of Jesus during mortality, they have the ongoing potential to be in the presence of His Spirit *every moment of their lives.* How casually we seem to treat this promise at times! Imagine if we had been there at Bountiful and witnessed the Savior's arrival. Surely none of us would have said, "Well, I'll stay here an hour or so, but then I'm going home to get some gardening done." Like the others there, we would have delighted in every single moment of His presence. Yet when it comes to the presence of the Holy Ghost, there are times when we seem to be less committed. We may think, for example, "I know this probably isn't the best movie, but there are just a few bad parts, and it's no worse than what I hear at work every day." We can choose to watch the movie, but the presence of the Holy Ghost will leave us for a while. If we truly understood the great privilege it is to have the Holy Ghost with us, we would avoid any behavior that would cause Him to leave. The companionship of the Holy Ghost in our lives will significantly help us align our wills with Heavenly Father's. Our patterns of behavior will be in greater harmony with His plan. Our prayers will focus on understanding His will for us. Our happiness will increase.

We should all thoughtfully prepare to participate in the sacrament each week. We will notice a change in our thoughts and behaviors as we keep the solemn sacramental promises. Our hearts and minds will turn to God more fully. Our motivation will become refined, and we will develop a greater desire for the things Heavenly Father wants for us. Furthermore, we will develop a greater understanding of His will for us. Partaking of the sacrament is a great opportunity to align our wills with God's.

Key Concept 7

Seek to have the constant companionship of the Holy Ghost through faithful adherence to covenants.

QUESTIONS FOR SELF-REFLECTION

- What does it mean to me to "take upon [me] the name of Christ"?
- Do I believe the Lord will answer my prayers?
- What am I willing to sacrifice to align my will with God's?
- How can prayer and scripture study help me better understand the Lord's specific will for me?

CHAPTER 10
"Awake, My Soul!"

OUR LIVES ARE GOING TO be difficult.

This is not a mistake, a flaw in the design, or the effect of a good plan gone awry. This is a fundamental purpose of our mortal experience. When we endure trials and suffering, Satan will try to convince us we have done something wrong. He will tell us we are not loved. But nothing could be further from the truth. Paul reminded the Hebrews, "And ye have forgotten the exhortation which speaketh unto you as unto children, My son, despise not thou the chastening of the Lord, nor faint when thou art rebuked of him: *for whom the Lord loveth he chasteneth, and scourgeth every son whom he receiveth*" (Hebrews 12:5–6; emphasis added).

I don't particularly like the sound of *chastening* or *rebuked* or *scourgeth*, and I presume no one really does. Yet I know Heavenly Father loves us. I know He wants us to be with Him again. He wants this so badly that He let His Only Begotten Son suffer and die to make this possible. If there is chastening or rebuking or scourging to come, it will come in the most loving and compassionate way possible. We must believe this, if only because to believe the opposite is to cast our Heavenly Father as an unkind or hostile parent. That simply isn't accurate.

Our Father in Heaven expects us to do our best. What does that mean? I honestly don't know for certain. It means something different for each person. It probably means something different for each person at each hour of each day. Some days our best is pretty good. Other days our best leaves a lot to be desired. I truly believe Heavenly Father accepts our offerings, as grand or as meager as they are, as long as we are trying. What does trying mean? It means we are moving forward, moving backward, making mistakes, making amends, committing sins, repenting, and trying to honor our covenants. It means we go to bed each night with godly sorrow for poor choices. It means we wake up each morning with a renewed determination to do better. Whether we improve ourselves or not that day is somewhat inconsequential, as long as we *tried*. If our best just wasn't good enough today, then we shouldn't worry. We need to keep trying. Our best will eventually be good enough, because that is the whole point of the Atonement of Jesus Christ. He will redeem us as we serve Him in faith.

Hope is when we not only believe something might happen, but when we have a strong desire for it to happen. It is a companion principle to faith and charity. It is essential in our progression toward eternal life. Mormon discussed this concept as follows:

> And again, my beloved brethren, I would speak unto you concerning hope. How is it that ye can attain unto faith, save ye shall have hope? And what is it that ye shall hope for? Behold I say unto you that ye shall have hope through the atonement of Christ and the power of his resurrection, to be raised unto life eternal, and this because of your faith in him according to the promise. (Moroni 7:40–41)

What do we hope for? We hope to live again after death. We hope to live forever with our Heavenly Father and our elder brother Jesus Christ. We *can* do this because of His Atonement. We *can* do this because of the Restoration of the gospel. We *can* do this because we will keep trying, day by day, to follow the Savior. President Dieter F. Uchtdorf explained the following regarding hope:

> We hope in Jesus the Christ, in the goodness of God, in the manifestations of the Holy Spirit, in the knowledge that prayers are heard and answered. Because God has been faithful and kept His promises in the past, we can hope with confidence that God will keep His promises to us in the present and in the future. In times of distress, we can hold tightly to the hope that things will "work together for [our] good" as we follow the counsel of God's prophets. This type of hope in God, His goodness, and His power refreshes us with courage during difficult challenges and gives strength to those who feel threatened by enclosing walls of fear, doubt, and despair.[20]

God loves us, and He keeps His promises. We can trust He will redeem us. His purpose is to help us live forever and partake of exaltation with Him (see Moses 1:39). Even in our darkest moments, when everyone else has failed us,

---

20   Dieter F. Uchtdorf, "The Infinite Power of Hope," *Ensign*, Nov. 2008, 23.

He will not fail us. This is why we can hope. This is our source of confidence. This is why we can pick ourselves up after every failure. This is why we can move forward with determination.

In the following example, the Savior teaches how much He loves and cares for us:

> And why take ye thought for raiment? Consider the lilies of the field, how they grow; they toil not, neither do they spin: And yet I say unto you, That even Solomon in all his glory was not arrayed like one of these. Wherefore, if God so clothe the grass of the field, which to day is, and to morrow is cast into the oven, shall he not much more clothe you, O ye of little faith? (Matthew 6:28–30)

The Savior is saying if God takes such great care to make a little flower so beautiful, won't He bless us even more? Flowers that live today and die tomorrow get attention from the Creator of the universe. What then of His children? His eternal sons and daughters? How much more will He clothe us, or sustain us, or bless us, or prosper us? He will, and He will do it with great abundance. He will do it even more as we increase our faith and obedience. What a marvelous blessing to be children of God and to have this brief time on earth to prepare to return unto Him.

In the midst of our trials, I offer the following counsel. Let's lift up our heads. Let's cast aside our self-doubts. We need to acknowledge our limitations but not be overwhelmed by them. We are children of the Most High God. We are younger siblings of the greatest man to have ever walked the earth. The most powerful beings in the universe love us deeply. They will do everything in their power to lead us to happiness.

> Therefore, fear not, little flock; do good; let earth and hell combine against you, for if ye are built upon my rock, they cannot prevail. Behold, I do not condemn you; go your ways and sin no more; perform with soberness the work which I have commanded you. *Look unto me in every thought; doubt not, fear not.* Behold the wounds which pierced my side, and also the prints of the nails in my hands and feet; be faithful, keep my commandments, and ye shall inherit the kingdom of heaven. Amen. (D&C 6:34–37; emphasis added)

As Nephi reflected on the goodness of God and the hope that comes from an accurate understanding of the gospel, he exclaimed,

> Rejoice, O my heart, and cry unto the Lord, and say: O Lord, I will praise thee forever; yea, my soul will rejoice in thee, my God, and the rock of my salvation . . . . therefore I will lift up my voice unto thee; yea, I will cry unto thee, my God, the rock of my righteousness. Behold, my voice shall forever ascend up unto thee, my rock and mine everlasting God. Amen. (2 Nephi 4:30, 35)

Any momentary grief was swallowed up in the joy that comes from knowing that with God, nothing is impossible.

I add my testimony to that of Nephi and the many others that have been provided herein. I know Heavenly Father lives and loves us. I know Jesus is the Christ. His powerful sacrifice is sufficient for all who will repent. It will help us become better and return to live with Him and our Father. May God bless us to realize our potential as sons and daughters of God. May we be filled with confidence to move forward. May the God of Heaven answer our prayers and fill us with the peace "which passeth all understanding" (Philippians 4:7).

ABOUT THE AUTHOR

David T. Morgan is a licensed psychologist with more than twenty years of experience in the mental health field. He has a BS in psychology, an MS in counseling and guidance, and a PhD in counseling psychology from Brigham Young University. He and his amazing wife are the parents of six children. David loves the scriptures and truly believes the answers to life's challenges can be found in the words of ancient and modern prophets. He also loves Disneyland and knows almost more about the Happiest Place on Earth than he does about psychology.